Financial Engineering and Risk Management — Vol. 1

ENTERPRISE
RISK
MANAGEMENT

Financial Engineering and Risk Management — Vol. 1

ENTERPRISE
RISK
MANAGEMENT

David L. Olson
University of Nebraska, USA

Desheng Dash Wu
University of Toronto, Canada

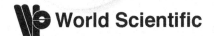 **World Scientific**

NEW JERSEY · LONDON · SINGAPORE · BEIJING · SHANGHAI · HONG KONG · TAIPEI · CHENNAI

Published by

World Scientific Publishing Co. Pte. Ltd.

5 Toh Tuck Link, Singapore 596224

USA office: 27 Warren Street, Suite 401-402, Hackensack, NJ 07601

UK office: 57 Shelton Street, Covent Garden, London WC2H 9HE

British Library Cataloguing-in-Publication Data
A catalogue record for this book is available from the British Library.

ENTERPRISE RISK MANAGEMENT

ISBN-13 978-981-279-148-1
ISBN-10 981-279-148-5

Printed in Singapore.

Preface

Enterprise risk management has always been important, at the heart of the insurance market during the age of sailing ships if not earlier. It has become a critically important topic in the last decade, expanding the scope of risk management beyond insurance and finance to include accounting risk (motivated in part by Enron and other problems), terrorism, and realization that many things can threaten an organization.

This book approaches risk management from five perspectives. In addition to the core perspective of financial risk management, we also address perspectives of accounting, supply chains, information systems, and disaster management. Risks are inherent in business. Without risk, there would be no motivation to conduct business. But a key principle is that organizations should accept those risks that they are competent to deal with, and "outsource" other risks to those (such as insurance companies) more competent to deal with them.

We also address tools available to assess risk, enabling better informed managerial decision making. These tools include balanced scorecards, multiple criteria analysis, simulation, data envelopment analysis, and financial risk measures.

The book concludes with a section of four cases. The first reviews how a Canadian organization developed their risk management structure, providing useful views of their approach in implementing risk management. Cases involving supply chain risk are reviewed, as well as cases involving enterprise resource planning systems in the information system field. The last case describes a Swedish exercise in disaster management, yielding insight into relative effectiveness of communication media in emergency environments.

David L. Olson
Desheng Wu

Contents

PART I: Perspectives

PART 1: Perspectives.

Chapter 1

Enterprise Risk Management

A description of ERM is provided, with subsequent chapters
providing:
> Financial perspectives
> Accounting perspectives
> Supply chain perspectives
> Information system perspectives
> Disaster management perspectives
Types of risk are reviewed
> In terms of opportunity
> Types of business risks
> Strategic risks
A risk management framework is reviewed

The concept of enterprise risk management (ERM) developed in the mid-1990s in industry, with a managerial focus. There are over 80 risk management frameworks reported worldwide, to include that of the Committee of Sponsoring Organizations of the Treadway Commission (COSO) 2004. COSO is a leading accounting standards organization in the U.S. ERM is a systematic, integrated approach to managing all risks facing an organization.[1] It focuses on board supervision, aiming to identify, evaluate, and manage all major corporate risks in an integrated framework.[2] It was undoubtedly encouraged by traumatic recent events such as 9/11/2001 and business scandals to include Enron and WorldCom.[3] A recent Tillinghast-Towers Perrin survey reported that nearly half of the insurance industry used an ERM process (with another 40 percent planning to do so), and 40 percent[4] had a chief risk officer.[5] But consideration of risk has always been with business, manifesting itself in medieval coffee houses such as Lloyd's of London, spreading risk related to cargos on the high seas.

The field of insurance developed to cover a wide variety of risks, related to external and internal risks covering natural catastrophes, accidents, human error, and even fraud. Financial risk has been controlled through hedge funds and other tools over the years, often by investment banks. With time, it was realized that many risks could be prevented, or their impact reduced, through loss-prevention and control systems, leading to a broader view of risk management.

Contingency management has been widely systematized in the military, although individual leaders have practiced various forms for millennia. Systematic organizational planning recently has been observed to include scenario analysis, giving executives a means of understanding what might go wrong, giving them some opportunity to prepare reaction plans. A complicating factor is that organization leadership is rarely a unified whole, but rather consists of a variety of stakeholders with potentially differing objectives.

Enterprise risks are inherently part of corporate strategy.[6] Thus consideration of risks in strategy selection can be one way to control them. ERM can be viewed as top-down by necessity for this reason. For example, currency risk arises because a company chose to involve itself in international activity. Divestment (and incorporation) often arises from desires to obtain legal protection as a means to reduce risk. An example was the formation of Alyeska Pipeline Service Company in 1970 to build and service the Alaska pipeline.

The book will look at risk management from five perspectives, each of which will be treated in a chapter in Part I. These perspectives are financial, accounting, supply chain, information system, and disaster management.

1.1 What is ERM?

Enterprise risk can include a variety of factors with potential impact on an organizations activities, processes, and resources. External factors can result from economic change, financial market developments, and dangers arising in political, legal, technological, and demographic environments. Risks can arise over time, as the public may change their views on products or practices such as:[7]

Automobile safety	Barbie dolls	Big box chain stores
Clothing from Third World factories	Corporate-owned farms	Disposable packaging
Executive salaries	Food additives	Furs
Hydroelectric dams	Logging	Nuclear power
Spanking	Sugar	Toy guns

Most of these are beyond the control of a given organization, although organizations can prepare and protect themselves in time-honored ways. Internal risks include human error, fraud, systems failure, disrupted production, and other risks. Often systems are assumed to be in place to detect and control risk, but inaccurate numbers are generated for various reasons.[8] Organizations of all types need robust, reliable systems to control risks that arise in all facets of life. Table 1 describes differences between ERM and traditional risk management:

Table 1: Differences between ERM and Traditional Risk Management[9]

Traditional Risk Management	ERM
Risk as individual hazards	Risk viewed in context of business strategy
Risk identification & assessment	Risk portfolio development
Focus on discrete risks	Focus on critical risks
Risk mitigation	Risk optimization
Risk limits	Risk strategy
Risks with no owners	Defined risk responsibilities
Haphazard risk quantification	Monitoring & measurement of risks
"Risk is not my responsibility"	"Risk is everyone's responsibility"

Tools of risk management can include creative risk financing solutions, blending financial, insurance and capital market strategies.[10] Capital market instruments include catastrophe bonds, risk exchange swaps, derivatives/options, catastrophe equity puts (cat-e-puts), contingent surplus notes, collateralized debt obligations, and weather derivatives.

1.2 Types of Risk

Risks can be viewed as threats, but businesses exist to cope with specific risks. Thus, if they encounter a risk that they are specialists in dealing with, the encounter is viewed as an opportunity. Risks have been categorized into five groups:[11]

1. **Opportunities** – events presenting a favorable combination of circumstances giving rise to the chance for beneficial activity;
2. **Killer risks** – events presenting an unfavorable combination of circumstances leading to hazard or major loss or damage resulting in permanent cessation of operations;
3. **Other perils** – events presenting an unfavorable combination of circumstances leading to hazard of loss or damage leading to disruption of operations with possible financial loss;
4. **Cross functional risks** – common risks leading to potential loss of reputation;
5. **Business process unique risks** – risks occurring within a specific operation or process, such as withdrawal of a particular product for quality reasons.

Opportunities should be capitalized upon in most circumstances. Not taking advantages of opportunities leads to growth of competitors, and thus increased risk. If opportunities are pursued, enterprise strategy can be modified to manage the particular risks involved. Killer risks are threats to enterprise survival, and call for continuous risk treatment, monitoring, and reporting. The other perils require analysis to assess ownership, treatment, residual risk, measurement, and reporting. Table 2 describes a variety of risk types faced by most organizations:

Table 2: Business Risk Types[12]

External Environment	Business Strategies & Policies	Business Process Execution

Competitors
Legal & regulatory
  Catastrophic loss
Medical cost / utilization
  trends
Customer expectations
	Strategy & innovation
	Capital allocation
	Business / product
	  portfolio
	Organization structure
	Organization policies
		Planning
		Process / technology
		  design
		Technology execution &
		  continuity
		Vendor / partner reliance
		Customer satisfaction
		Regulatory compliance &
		  privacy
		Knowledge / intellectual
		  capital
		Change integration

People	**Analysis & Reporting**	**Technology & Data**

Leadership
Skills / competency
Change readiness
Communication
Performance incentives
Accountability
Fraud & abuse
	Performance
	  management
	Budgeting / financial
	  planning
	Accounting / tax
	  information
	External reporting &
	  disclosure
	Pricing / margin
	Market intelligence
	Contract commitment
		Technology infrastructure /
		  architecture
		Data relevance & integrity
		Data processing integrity
		Technology reliability &
		  recovery
		IT security

This classification was for the healthcare industry, but demonstrates the scope of risks that organizations can face. The idea of enterprise risk management is to identify important risks for the organization, and develop strategies to deal with them.

1.2.1 *Strategic risks*

Risk strategy defines means of coping with risks, defining approaches to be adopted. If risks are in the organizations area of expertise, they become business opportunities. Risk strategies should establish guidelines to include:[13]

- Organization & responsibilities;
- Organizational risk attitude;
- Ownership for specific risks;
- Methods to be used at each planning level to deal with risk;
- Peer reviewing and benchmarking;
- Encouragement of proactive risk reporting;
- Criteria for risk assessment and definition of critical risks;
- Encouraging effective communication of risks.

If risks are not in areas where the organization has expert ability to cope, they should be defended against. Table 3 gives seven major strategic risk classes identified by a Harvard Business Review paper.

1.2.2 *A framework for risk management*

Risk management frameworks are designed to enable organizations to systematically cope with these risks. One enterprise operational framework is given below:[14]

Step 1: Establish a risk management framework

This step involves identifying evaluating, exploiting, financing, and monitoring risk events with the intent of focusing on value of the enterprise. It is related to establishment of strategic objectives. Top management is responsible to direct and set controls after consulting with stakeholders, and to constantly monitor operations with the intent of reducing risk and prioritizing strategic risks. It is often found beneficial to appoint a chief risk officer as a risk management champion.

Table 3: Strategic Risk Classes and Possible Defenses[15]

Strategic Risk	Example	Defense
Industry margin squeeze	Pharmaceuticals Cost escalation – semiconductors Airline deregulation Cycle volatility	*Shift the compete / collaborate ratio* Supply chain coordination, asset-sharing agreements, collaborative marketing
Technology shift	Loss of patent protection Outdated manufacturing processes	*Double bet* OS / 2 & Windows Analog & digital cellular
Brand erosion	Perrier contamination Firestone & Ford Explorer GM Saturn	*Redefine brand investment scope* Redesign service, quality *Reallocate brand investment* AMEX response to VISA
One-of-a-kind competitor	Wal-Mart	*Create new non-overlapping business design* Target – Family Dollar Stores
Customer priority shift	Bottled Water – Pepsi & Coke	*Early detection* *Fast & cheap experimentation* Capital One
New project failure	Edsel	*Smart sequencing* Do better-understood, controllable first *Develop excess options* *Stepping-stone method* Series of projects
Market stagnation		*Generate demand-innovation*

Step 2: Risk requirements

The intent is to understand organizational internal and external key stakeholders and their objectives and strategies with respect to risk. Establishment of risk requirements includes assessment, to include analysis and evaluation. Required data needs to be identified, along with the reason for collecting it. Risk exposure is measured through risk models. Two broad measures in enterprise risk management are solvency-related and performance-related. Solvency-related measures focus on financial measures such as value at risk and shortfall risk. Performance-related risk includes cause and effect models to assess the effect of decisions, such as a pro forma projections contingent upon some hazardous event occurring.

Step 3: Identify the flow of information

Threats and opportunities need to be reported. An accurate and detailed flowchart of information flow as well as the software and hardware needed by each department or location is needed, along with identification of skilled personnel required to operate them.

Step 4: Feasibility analysis

Alternative means of obtaining risk management software should be identified. The cost of the proposed system is estimated, along with system purpose and users. The ability to cope with increased work load also needs to be considered.

Step 5: Buy or lease

After feasibility analysis, decisions need to be made.. There are many companies offering customized packages for specific aspects of risk management, to include financial management, insurance risk, project risk, and risks in specific industries.

After risks are treated, residual reporting of treatment effectiveness is needed, monitoring the effectiveness of treatments.

1.3 Current Status

The Conference Board published results of a survey of 271 risk management executives from North America and Europe.[16] Respondents of organizations with long ERM experience indicated that ERM had significantly added higher levels of value to organizations than did those respondents belonging to organizations that had implemented ERM more recently. Benefits cited were better-informed decisions (86 percent of experienced ERM organizations; 58 percent of all others), greater management consensus (83 percent of experienced, 36 percent of all others), and increased management accountability (79 percent of experienced, 34 percent of all others). Those organizations that had fully implemented ERM were better able to accomplish strategic planning, and had a stronger ability to understand and weigh risk tradeoffs.

There has been significant recent research into the use of ERM,[17] to include reports of the uses of ERM by Canadian risk and insurance management companies.[18] One study reported results of a survey of 52 companies with respect to risk management practices.[19] Results of a survey of 123 organizations found the following variables positively related to ERM implementation: presence of a chief risk officer, board independence, top management support, presence of a Big Four auditor, entity size, and the industries of banking, education, and insurance.[20] All studies indicate a great deal of interest in ERM, with less than 20 percent of surveyed organizations not interested in it. The formal implementation of ERM is clearly growing, driven in part by risk management professional organizations.

Stroh (2005) reviewed the process of ERM at UnitedHealth Management (UHM). UHM is a large, diversified company dedicated to making the healthcare system work better. HRM serves the healthcare industry with benefits, services, and analytic tools aimed at improving clinical and financial performance. UHM viewed ERM as a discipline embedded within the organizational philosophy, meant to identify business risk factors, assess their severity, quantify them, and mitigate them while capitalizing on upside opportunities. A pyramid of risks was given as in Table 4:

Table 4: Risks by Level[21]

Top level	Strategic business risk	Decompose strategic risks / opportunities Mitigation / acceleration plan Assure leadership that top risks are in sight
2nd level	Market / business environment risk	Internal risk sensing (identify potential issues early & alert management) External risk sensing (peer, industry, market monitoring)
3rd level	Financial performance risk	Identify gaps in management plans to achieve financial targets Test / verify assumptions behind key decisions
4th level	Operational risk	Develop baseline, audit plan to link strategic & tactical risks Provide advisory services to develop operational controls
5th level	Compliance and financial reporting risk	Partner with external audit General & regular financial controls

ERM was viewed as providing UHM a framework for discipline, a methodology enabling management to effectively deal with uncertainty and associated risks.

1.4 Conclusions

We have given a brief initial description of ERM. That process begins by identifying risks specific to an organization. There are many types of risk that can affect a business (or any organization for that matter). A systematic approach to risk can lead to more rational organizational management.

While risk needs to be managed, taking risks is fundamental to doing business. Profit by necessity requires accepting some risk. ERM seeks to provide means to recognize and mitigate risks, and provides tools to rationally manage these risks. Businesses exist to cope with specific risks efficiently. Uncertainty creates opportunities for businesses to make profits.

There are many perspectives to enterprise risk management. We will review financial, accounting, supply chain operations, information system, and disaster planning perspectives in chapters to follow in this section. Then in part 2 we will present some modeling methods that can support decision making in the enterprise risk management decision arena. Part 3 will conclude the book with cases of modeling applied to risk management applications.

Endnotes

1. Dickinson, G. (2001). Enterprise risk management: Its origins and conceptual foundation, *The Geneva Papers on Risk and Insurance* 26:3, 360-366.
2. Gates, S., Nanes, A. (2006). Incorporating strategic risk into enterprise risk management: A survey of current corporate practice, *Journal of Applied Corporate Finance* 18:4, 81-90.
3. Walker, L., Shenkir, W.G., Barton, T.L. (2003). ERM in practice 60:4, 51-55; Baranoff, E.G. (2004). Risk management: A focus on a more holistic approach three years after September 11, *Journal of Insurance Regulation* 22:4, 71-81.
4. Sereda, H. Gaudio, D. Tait, E. (2005) RMIS: Taking data management enterprisewide, *Risk Management Magazine* October, 42-52.
5. Miccolis, J. (2002). Insurers and ERM: Working on the how, *National Underwriter/Property & Casualty Risk & Benefits Management* 107:14, 36-37.
6. Dickinson (2001), op cit.
7. Pinker, S. (2002). *The Blank Slate: The Modern Denial of Human Nature*. London: Penguin Books.
8. Schaefer, A, Cassidy, M., Marshall, K., Rossi, J. (2006), Internal audits and executive education: A holy alliance to reduce theft and misreporting, *Employee Relations Law Journal* 32:1, 61-84.

9. Table developed from information provided by Banham, R. (2004). Enterprising views of risk management, *Journal of Accountancy* 197:6, 65-71.
10. Baranoff (2004), op cit.
11. Drew, M. (2007). Information risk management and compliance – Expect the unexpected, *BT Technology Journal* 25:1, 19-29.
12. Table developed from information provided by Stroh, P.J. (2005). Enterprise risk management at United Health Group, *Strategic Finance* 87:1, 27-35.
13. Drew (2007), op cit.
14. Sereda et al. (2005), op cit.
15. Slywotzky, A.J. Drzik, J. (2005). Countering the biggest risk of all, *Harvard Business Review* April, 78-88.
16. Millage, A. (2005). ERM is still in its infancy, *Internal Auditor*, 62:5, 16-17.
17. Walker et al. (2003), op cit.
18. Kleffner, A.E., Lee, R.B., McGannon, B. (2003). The effect of corporate governance on the use of enterprise risk management: Evidence from Canada, *Risk management & Insurance Review* 6:1, 53-73.
19. Lynch-Bell, M. (2002). Taking a risk with shareholder value, *Chemical Engineer* 732, 18.
20. Beasley, M.S., Clune, R., Hermanson, D.R. (2005). ERM: A status report, Internal Auditor 62:1, 67-72.
21. Table developed from information provided by Stroh, P.J. (2005), op cit.

Chapter 2

The Financial Perspective

Discusses the relationship between ERM and financial operations
Describes two market risk measures
    Variance at risk
    Scenario analysis
Discusses factors of credit risk measurement
Reviews event types in the Basel II accords

Recent financial disasters in financial and non-financial firms and in governmental agencies have led to increased emphasis on various forms of risk management such as market risk management, credit risk management, and operational risk management. Financial institutions like banks are further motivated by the need to meet various regulatory requirements for risk measurement and capital. There is an increasing tendency toward an integrated or holistic view of risks. A framework for thinking about the collective risk of a group of financial instruments and an individual security's contribution to that collective risk would be useful. A Tillinghast-Towers Perrin survey has reported that nearly half of the insurance industry used an integrated risk management process (with another 40 percent planning to do so), and 40 percent had a chief risk officer.[1]

Enterprise Risk Management (ERM) is an integrated approach to achieving the enterprise's strategic, programmatic, and financial objectives with acceptable risk. The philosophy of ERM generalizes these concepts beyond financial risks to include all kinds of risks. For example, a portfolio of equity investments has been generalized to the entire collection of risks facing an organization. A number of principles have often been found useful in practice:

1. Portfolio risk can never be the simple sum of various individual risk elements.
2. One has to understand various individual risk elements and their interactions in order to understand portfolio risk.
3. The key risk, i.e., the most important risk, contributes most to the portfolio risk or the risk facing the entire organization. Therefore, decision makers should be most concerned about key risk decisions.
4. Using quantitative approaches to measure risk is very important. For example, a key financial market risk can broadly be defined as volatility relative to the capital markets. One measure of this risk is the cost of capital, which can be measured through models such as the Weighted Average Cost of Capital (WACC) and Capital Asset Pricing Model (CAPM).[2]

2.1 ERM and Financial Operations

Traditional finance operations have focused on cost and efficiency in operations and processes.[3] A firm is assumed to seek efficiency either through information technologies such as enterprise systems, or through newer operations management techniques such as shared cost/services and outsourcing. While this has been sufficient to preserve competitive advantage when these methods were novel and not widely used, use by competitors makes heavy investment in information technology highly risky. Companies, financial or not, have achieved high performance by utilizing information technology to capture and process data. The challenge today is to process the inherent uncertainties of business, in this case, through finance operations data, in order to develop a coherent strategy. Efficiency is a means to achieve strategic objectives. Where there is strategy, there is an attempt to overcome uncertainty and incomplete knowledge, to act in the face of risk.

To make clear where ERM takes over from finance operations, we must examine best and first principles. While finance operations in an enterprise vary across different industries and products and services provided, effective finance operations rely on four competencies: (1) Transaction processing: creating satisfied efficiency in core finance functions, e.g., accounts payable and general ledger which are increasingly delivered through shared services or outsourcing strategies. (2) Financial and regulatory reporting: capturing regulatory and tax reporting requirements from a transactional and systems perspective. (3) Management reporting: providing various data and information for management decision making, and (4) Internal controls: providing support to effective risk management within the enterprise through the disciplined oversight of financial, accounting and audit systems.

These four competencies are similar to the COSO ERM framework,[4] where three objective categories are identified: operational objectives, financial reporting objectives, and compliance objectives. The COSO framework defines ERM as an ongoing process for identifying and managing potential events and operations that could affect the entity's ability to manage business risks such that they remain within its risk appetite.[5]

Finance operational activities are usually managed through various quantitative models that can be used by ERM. Value-at-Risk models have been popular, partially in response to Basel II banking guidelines.[6] Other analytic approaches include simulation of internal risk rating systems using past data and decision analysis models.[7] Swedish banks have been found to use credit rating categories, and that each bank reflected its own risk policy.[8] One bank was found to have a higher level of defaults, but without adversely affecting profitability due to constraining high risk loans to low amounts. Systemic risk from overall economic systems as well as risk from networks of banks with linked loan portfolios are important.[9] Overall economic system risk was found to be much more likely, while linked loan portfolios involved high impact but very low probability of default.[10]

2.1.1 *Key financial risks*

Typically, the major sources of value loss in financial institutions are identified as:

- *Market risk* is exposure to the uncertain market value of a portfolio, where the underlying economic factors are such as interest rates, exchange rates, and equity and commodity prices.
- *Credit risk* is the risk that a counterparty may be unable to perform on an obligation.
- *Operational risk* is the risk of loss resulting from inadequate or failed internal processes, people and systems, or from external events. The committee indicates that this definition excludes systemic risk, legal risk and reputational risk.[11]

During the early part of the 1990s, much of the focus was on techniques for measuring and managing market risk. As the decade progressed, this shifted to techniques of measuring and managing credit risk. By the end of the decade, firms and regulators were increasingly focusing on Operational risk.

2.1.2 *Measuring market risk*

A trader holds a portfolio of commodity forwards. She knows what its market value is today, but she is uncertain as to its market value a week from today. She faces market risk. The trader employs the derivatives "greeks" to describe and to characterize the various exposures to fluctuations in financial prices inherent in a particular position or portfolio of instruments. Such a portfolio of instruments may include cash instruments, derivatives instruments, borrowing and lending. In this article, we will introduce two additional techniques for measuring and reporting risk: Value-at-Risk assessment and scenario analysis.

Market risk is concerned both internally and externally. Internally, managers and traders in financial service industry need a measure that allows active, efficient management of the firm's risk position. Externally, regulators want to be sure a financial company's potential for catastrophic net worth loss is accurately measured and that the company's economic capital is sufficient to survive such a loss. Although both managers and regulators want up-to-date measures of risk, they do estimate exposure to risks based on different time horizons. Bank managers and traders measures market risks on a daily basis, which is very costly and time consuming. Thus, bank managers compromise between measurement precision on the one hand and the cost and timeliness of reporting on the other.

Regulators are concerned with the maximum loss a bank is likely to experience over a given horizon so that they can set the bank's required capital (i.e. its economic net worth) to be greater than the estimated maximum loss and be almost sure that the bank will not fail over that horizon. As a result, they are concerned with the overall riskiness of a bank and have less concern with the risk of individual portfolio components.[12] The time horizon used in computation is relatively long. For example, Under Basel II capital for market risk is based on the 10-day 99% VaR and for credit risk and operational risk is based on a one-year 99.9% VaR.

2.2 Market Risk Measurements

There are two principle approaches to risk measurement: value-at-risk analysis and scenario analysis.

2.2.1 *VaR – Value at risk*

Value at Risk, or VaR, represents a measure of the risk inherent in a portfolio of financial instruments or contracts, such as a trading portfolio. It can be characterised as a maximum expected loss, given some time horizon and within a given confidence interval. Its utility is in providing a measure of risk that illustrates the risk inherent in a portfolio with multiple risk factors, such as portfolios held by large banks, which are diversified across many risk factors and product types. The VaR and other analytics are primarily run in a series of overnight, automated batch processes. The flow of information and processing is roughly as outlined in Figure 1:

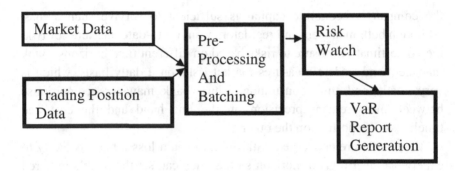

Figure 1: Information Flow and Processing

VaR is a measure of risk that is globally accepted by regulatory bodies responsible for supervision of banking activities. These regulatory bodies, in broad terms, enforce regulatory practices as outlined by the Basel Committee on Banking Supervision of the Bank for International Settlements (BIS). The regulator that has responsibility for financial institutions in Canada is the Office of the Superintendent of Financial Institutions (OSFI), and OSFI typically follows practices and criteria as proposed by the Basel Committee.

A key agreement of the Basel Committee is the Basel Capital Accord (generally referred to as "Basel" or the "Basel Accord"), which has been updated several times since 1988. From the point of view of Market Risk Operations, the most significant Amendment to the Basel Accord occurred in January 1996.

In the 1996 (updated, 1998) Amendment to the Basel Accord, banks are encouraged to use internal models to measure Value at Risk, and the numbers produced by these internal models support capital charges to ensure the capital adequacy, or liquidity, of the bank. Some elements of the minimum standard established by Basel are:

- VaR should be computed daily, using a 99th percentile, one-tailed confidence interval
- A minimum price shock equivalent to ten trading days be used. This is called the "holding period" and simulates a 10-day period of liquidating assets in a period of market crisis

- The model should incorporate a historical observation period of at least one year
- The capital charge is set at a minimum of three times the average of the daily value-at-risk of the preceding 60 business days

In practice, these minimum standards mean that the VaR that is produced by the Market Risk Operations area is multiplied first by the square root of 10 (to simulate 10 days holding) and then multiplied by a minimum capital multiplier of 3 to establish capital held against regulatory requirements.

In summary, VaR provides the worst expected loss at the 99% confidence level. That is, a 99% confidence interval produces a measure of loss that will be exceeded only 1% of the time. But this does mean there will likely be a larger loss than the VaR calculation two or three times in a year. This is compensated for by the inclusion of the multiplicative factors, above, and the implementation of Stress Testing, which falls outside the scope of the activities of Market Risk Operations.

Various approaches can be used to compute VaR, of which three are widely used: Historical Simulation, Variance-covariance approach, and Monte Carlo simulation. Variance-covariance approach is used for investment portfolios, but it does not usually work well for portfolios involving options that are close to delta neutral. Monte Carlo simulation solves the problem of non-linearity approximation if model error is not significant, but it suffers some technical difficulties such as how to deal with time-varying parameters and how to generate maturation values for instruments that mature before the VaR horizon. We present Historical Simulation and Variance-covariance approach in the following two sections. Regarding the steps to implement *Monte Carlo* simulation, Please refer to Chapter 9 of this book.

2.2.2 *Historical simulation*

Historical simulation is a good tool to estimate VAR in most banks. Observations of day-over-day changes in market conditions are captured. These market conditions are represented using upwards of 100,000 points daily of observed and implied Market Data. This historical market data is captured and used to generate historical 'shocks' to current spot market data. This shocked market data is used to price the Bank's trading positions as against changing market conditions, and these revalued positions then are compared against the base case (using spot data). This simulates a theoretical profit or loss. Each day of historically observed data produces a theoretical profit/loss number in this way, and all of these theoretical P&L numbers produce a distribution of theoretical profits/losses. The (1-day) VaR can then be read as the 99th percentile of this distribution.

A brief comment should be made regarding the advantages/ disadvantages of historical simulation. The primary advantage is ease of use and implementation. In Market Risk Operations, historical data is collected and reviewed on a regular basis, before it is added to the historical data set. Since this data corresponds to historical events, it can be reviewed in a straightforward manner. Also, the historical nature of the data allows for some clarity of explanation of VaR numbers. For instance, the Bank's VaR may be driven by widening credit spreads, or by decreasing equity volatilities, or both, and this will be visible in actual historical data. Additionally, historical data implicitly contains correlations and non-linear effects (e.g. gamma, vega and cross-effects).

The most obvious disadvantage of historical simulation is the assumption that the past presents a reasonable simulation of future events. Additionally, a large bank usually holds a large portfolio, and there can be considerable operational overhead involved in producing a VaR against a large portfolio with dependencies on a large and varied number of model inputs. All the same, other VaR methods, such as variance-covariance (VCV) and Monte Carlo simulation, produce essentially the same objections. The main alternative to historical simulation is to make assumptions about the probability distributions of the returns on the market variables and calculate the probability distribution of the change in the value of the portfolio analytically. This is known as the variance-covariance approach. VCV is a parametric approach and contains the assumption of normality, and the assumption of the stability of correlation and at the same time. Monte Carlo simulation provides another tool to these two methods. Monte Carlo methods are dependent on decisions regarding model calibration, which have effectively the same problems. No VaR methodology is without simplifying assumptions, and several different methods are in use at institutions worldwide. The literature on volatility estimation is large and seemingly subject to unending growth, especially in acronyms.[13]

2.2.3 *Variance-covariance approach*

VCV Models portfolio returns as a multivariate normal distribution. We can use a position vector containing cash flow present values to represent all components of the portfolio and describe the portfolio. VCV approach concerns most the return and covariance matrix(Q) representing the risk attributes of the portfolio over the chosen horizon. The standard deviation of portfolio value (σ), also called volatility, is computed:

$$\sigma = \sqrt{h'Qh} \tag{1}$$

The volatility (σ) is then scaled to find the desired centile of portfolio value that is the predicted maximum loss for the portfolio or VaR:

$$VaR = \sigma f(Y)$$
$$where: \quad f(Y) \text{ is the scale factor for centile } Y. \tag{2}$$

For example, for a multivariate normal return distribution, $f(Y) = 2.33$ for $Y = 1\%$.

It is then easy to calculate VaR from the standard deviation (1-day VaR = 2.33s). The simplest assumption is that daily gains/losses are normally distributed and independent. The N-day VaR equals $\sqrt{N}$ times the one-day VaR. When there is autocorrelation equal to r the multiplier is increased from N to

$$N + 2(N-1)\rho + 2(N-2)\rho^2 + 2(N-3)\rho^3 + \ldots 2\rho^{n-1}$$

Besides being easy to compute, VCV also lends itself readily to the calculation of the calculation of the marginal risk (Marginal VaR), Incremental VaR and Component VaR of candidate trades. For a Portfolio where an amount x_i is invested in the ith component of the portfolio, these three VaR measures are computed as:

- Marginal VaR: $\dfrac{\partial \text{VaR}}{\partial x_i}$

- Incremental VaR: Incremental effect of ith component on VaR

- Component VaR $x_i \dfrac{\partial \text{VaR}}{\partial x_i}$

VCV uses delta-approximation, which means the representative cash flow vector is a linear approximation of positions. In some cases, a second-order term in the cash flow representation is included to improve this approximation.[14] However, this does not always improve the risk estimate and can only be done with the sacrifice of some of the computational efficiency. In general, VCV works well in calculating linear instruments such as forward, interest rate SWAP, but works quite badly in non-linear instruments such as various options.

2.2.4 *Scenario analysis*

Scenario analysis typically refers to varying a wider range of parameters at the same time. Scenario analyses often examine the impact of catastrophic events on the firm's financial position, for example, simultaneous movements in a number of risk categories affecting all of a firm's business operations, such as business volumes, investment values and interest rate movements. Scenarios can also be generally considered under three broad headings. Changes to the business plan, changes in business cycles and those relating to extreme events. The scenarios can be derived in a variety of ways including stochastic models or a repetition of an historical event. Scenarios can be developed with varying degrees of precision and depth. One specific scenario analysis is Stress testing, which typically refers to shifting the values of individual parameters that affect the financial position of a firm, and then determining the effect on the firm's business. A stress test isolates the impact on a portfolio's value of one or more predefined moves in a particular market risk factor or a small number of closely linked market risk factors. This approach has the advantage of not requiring a distributional assumption for the risk calculation. Scenario analyses are based on the analysis of the impact of unlikely, but not impossible, events. These events can be financial, operational, legal or relate to any other risk that might have an economic impact on the firm.

Because there is generally more focus on the specific question, stress and scenario tests can generally be constructed and get to the point of producing reliable results much more quickly than in the case for stochastic models. The actual scenarios used will be comprehensible to management of the business, and the subjectivity in the assessment of relative likelihood will clear for all to see.[15]

2.3 Measuring Credit Risk

Credit risks are defined as the risk of loss due to a debtor's non-payment of a loan or other line of credit (either the principal or interest (coupon) or both). Examples of Credit Risk Factors in the insurance industry are:

- Adequacy of reinsurance program for the risks selected
- Reinsurance failure of the company's reinsurance programme and the impact on claim recoveries
- Credit deterioration of the company's reinsurers, intermediaries or other counterparties
- Credit concentration to a single counterparty or group
- Credit concentration to reinsurers of particular rating grades
- Reinsurance rates increasing
- Bad Debts greater than expected.

A financial service firm has used a number of methods, e.g., credit scoring, ratings, credit committees, to assess the creditworthiness of counter-parties (Refer to Chapter 10 for details of these methods). This would make it difficult for the firm to integrate this source of risk with the market risks. Many financial companies are aware of the need for parallel treatment of all measurable risks and are doing something about it.[16]

If financial companies can "score" loans, they can determine how loan values change as scores change. Then, a probability distribution of value changes can be modeled relating to these changes produce over time due to credit risk. Finally, the time series of credit risk changes could be related to the market risk, which enable market risk and credit risk to be integrated into a single estimate of value change over a given horizon.

2.4 Measuring Operational Risk

"Operational risk is the risk of loss resulting from inadequate or failed internal processes, people, and systems, or from external events". The definition includes people risks, technology and processing risks, physical risks, legal risks, etc, but excludes reputation risk and strategic risk. The Operational Risk Management framework should include identification, measurement, monitoring, reporting, control and mitigation frameworks for Operational Risk. Basel II proposed three alternatives to measure operational risks: (1) Basic Indicator, which requires Financial Institutions to reserve 15% of annual gross income; (2) Standardized Approach, which is based on annual revenue of each of the broad business lines of the Financial Institution; and (3) Advanced Measurement Approach (AMA), which is based on the internally developed risk measurement framework of the bank adhering to the standards prescribed.

The following lists the official Basel II defined business lines:

- Corporate finance
- Trading and sales
- Retail banking

- Commercial banking
- Payment and settlement
- Agency services
- Asset management
- Retail brokerage

The following lists the official Basel II defined event types with some examples for each category:

- Internal Fraud - misappropriation of assets, tax evasion, intentional mismarking of positions, bribery: Loss due to acts of a type intended to defraud, misappropriate property or circumvent regulations, the law or company policy, excluding diversity/discrimination events, which involves at least one internal party.
- External Fraud - theft of information, hacking damage, third-party theft and forgery: Losses due to acts of a type intended to defraud, misappropriate property or circumvent the law, by a third party.
- Employment Practices and Workplace Safety - discrimination, workers compensation, employee health and safety: Losses arising from acts inconsistent with employment, health or safety laws or agreements, from payment of personal injury claims, or from diversity/discrimination events.
- Clients, Products, & Business Practice - market manipulation, antitrust, improper trade, product defects, fiduciary breaches, account churning; Losses arising from an unintentional or negligent failure to meet a professional obligation to specific clients (including fiduciary and suitability requirements), or from the nature or design of a product.
- Damage to Physical Assets - natural disasters, terrorism, vandalism: Losses arising from loss or damage to physical assets from natural disaster or other events.
- Business Disruption & Systems Failures - utility disruptions, software failures, hardware failures: Losses arising from disruption of business or system failures.

- Execution, Delivery, & Process Management - data entry errors, accounting errors, failed mandatory reporting, negligent loss of client assets: Losses from failed transaction processing or process management, from relations with trade counterparties and vendors

The Basel Committee breaks down loss events into seven general categories, given in Table 1:

Table 1: Loss Event Activities

Event-Type Category (Level 1)	Categories (Level 2)	Activities Examples (Level 3)
Internal Fraud	Unauthorized Activity	■ Transactions not reported (intentional) ■ Transaction type unauthorized (with monetary loss) ■ Mismarking of position (intentional)
"	Theft and Fraud	■ Fraud / credit fraud / worthless deposits ■ Theft / extortion / embezzlement / robbery ■ Misappropriation of assets ■ Forgery ■ Check kiting ■ Smuggling ■ Account take-over / impersonation, etc. ■ Tax non-compliance / evasion (willful) ■ Bribes / kickbacks ■ Insider trading (not on firm's account)
External Fraud	Theft and Fraud	■ Theft / robbery ■ Forgery ■ Check kiting
"	Systems Security	■ Hacking damage ■ Theft of information (with monetary loss)

Source: Basel Committee[17]

Table 1: Loss Event Activities (part 2)

Event-Type Category (Level 1)	Categories (Level 2)	Activities Examples (Level 3)
Employment Practices and Workplace Safety	Employee Relations	▪ Compensation, benefit, termination issues ▪ Organized labor activities
"	Safe Environment	▪ General liability (slips and falls, etc.) ▪ Employee health & safety rules and events ▪ Workers compensation
"	Diversity & Discrimination	▪ All discrimination types
Clients, Products & Business Practice	Suitability, Disclosure & Fiduciary	▪ Fiduciary breaches / guideline violations ▪ Suitability / disclosure issues (KYC, etc.) ▪ Retail consumer disclosure violations ▪ Breach of privacy ▪ Aggressive sales ▪ Account churning ▪ Misuse of confidential information ▪ Lender liability
"	Improper Business or Market Practices	▪ Antitrust ▪ Improper trade / market practice ▪ Market manipulation ▪ Insider trading (on firm's account) ▪ Unlicensed activity ▪ Money laundering
"	Product Flaws	▪ Product defects (unauthorized, etc.) ▪ Model errors
"	Selection, Sponsorship & Exposure	▪ Failure to investigate client per guidelines ▪ Exceeding client exposure limits
"	Advisory Activities	▪ Disputes over performance or advisory activities

Table 1: Loss Event Activities (part 3)

Event-Type Category (Level 1)	Categories (Level 2)	Activities Examples (Level 3)
Damage to Physical Assets	Disasters and Other Events	■ Natural disaster losses ■ Human losses from external sources (terrorism, vandalism)
Business Disruption & Systems Failures	Systems	■ Hardware ■ Software ■ Telecommunications ■ Utility outage / disruptions
Execution, Delivery & Process Management	Transaction Capture, Execution & Maintenance	■ Miscommunication ■ Data entry, maintenance or loading error ■ Missed deadline or responsibility ■ Model / system misoperation ■ Accounting error / entity attribution error ■ Other task misperformance ■ Delivery failure ■ Collateral management failure ■ Reference data maintenance
"	Monitoring & Reporting	■ Failed mandatory reporting obligation ■ Inaccurate external report (loss incurred)
"	Customer Intake & Documentation	■ Client permissions / disclaimers missed ■ Legal documents missing / incomplete
"	Customer / Client Account Management	■ Unapproved access given to accounts ■ Incorrect client records (loss incurred) ■ Negligent loss or damage of client assets
"	Trade Counterparties	■ Non-client counterparty misperformance ■ Misc. non-client counterparty disputes
"	Vendors & Suppliers	■ Outsourcing ■ Vendor disputes

Financial Institutions need to estimate their exposure to each type of risk for each business line combination. Ideally this will lead to $7 \times 8 = 56$ VaR measures that can be combined into an overall VaR measure. Other techniques to measure operational risks includes: Scenario Analysis, Identifying Causal Relationships, key risk indicator (KRI), Scorecard approaches, etc.

2.5 Conclusions

Risks in a financial firm can be quantified and managed using various models. Models also provide support to organizations seeking to control enterprise risk. ERM provides tools to integrate enterprise-wide operations and finance functions and better inform strategic decisions. The promise of ERM lies in allowing managers to better understand and use their firms' fundamental relation to uncertainty in a scientific framework: from each risk, strategy may create opportunity. We have discussed various risk modeling and reviewed some common risk measures in financial service company. We have demonstrated how different risk measures in ERM acts to integrate operation and finance functions, and effective control of work through a manufacturing system.

Endnotes

1. Walker, L., Shenkir, W.G., Barton, T.L. (2003). ERM in practice 60:4, 51-55; Baranoff, E.G. (2004). Risk management: A focus on a more holistic approach three years after September 11, *Journal of Insurance Regulation* 22:4, 71-81.
2. Sharpe, W.F. (1964). Capital asset prices: A theory of market equilibrium under conditions of risk, Journal of Finance, 19(3), 425-442.
3. Donnellan M., Sutcliff, M. (2006). *CFO Insights: Delivering High Performance*, John Wiley & Sons
4. Levinsohn, A. (2004). How to manage risk – Enterprise-wide, *Strategic Finance* 86(5), 55-56.

5. Committee of Sponsoring Organizations of the Treadway Commission (COSO), Enterprise risk management — integrated framework, American Institute of Certified Public Accountants, Jersey City, NJ. 2004.
6. Alexander, G.J., Baptista, A.M. (2004). A comparison of VaR and CVaR constraints on portfolio selection with the mean-variance model. *Management Science* 50(9), 1261-1273; Chavez-Demoulin, V., Embrechts, P., Nešlehová, J. (2006). Quantitative models for operational risk: Extremes, dependence and aggregation. *Journal of Banking & Finance* 30, 2635-2658.
7. Florez-Lopez, R. (2007). Modelling of insurers' rating determinants. An application of machine learning techniques and statistical models. *European Journal of Operational Research*, 183, 1488-1512
8. Jacobson, T., Lindé, J., Roszbach, K. (2006). Internal ratings systems, implied credit risk and the consistency of banks' risk classification policies. *Journal of Banking & Finance* 30, 1899-1926.
9. Elsinger, H., Lehar, A., Summer, M. (2006). Risk assessment for banking systems. *Management Science* 52(9), 1301-1314.
10. Crouhy, M., Galai, D. Mark, R. (2000). A comparative analysis of current credit risk models, *Journal of Banking & Finance* 24, 59-117; Crouhy, M., Galai, D., Mark, R. (1998). Model Risk, *Journal of Financial Engineering* 7(3/4), 267-288, reprinted in Model Risk: Concepts, Calibration and Pricing, (ed. R. Gibson), *Risk Book*, 2000, 17-31; Crook J. N., Edelman, D.B., Thomas, L.C. (2007). Recent developments in consumer credit risk assessment. *European Journal of Operational Research*, 183, 1447-146.
11. Basel Committee on Banking Supervision (June 2004). International Convergence of Capital Measurement and Capital Standards, Bank for International Settlements.
12. Pritsker, M. (1996). Evaluating value at risk methodologies: accuracy versus computational time, unpublished working paper, Board of Governors of the Federal Reserve System
13. Danielson, J., de Vries, C.G. (1997). Extreme returns, tail estimation, and value-at-risk. Working Paper, University of Iceland (http://www.hag.hi.is/~jond/research); Fallon, W. (1996).

Calculating value-at-risk. Working Paper, Columbia University (bfallon@groucho.gsb.columbia.edu); Garman, M.B. (1996). Improving on VaR. *Risk* 9, No. 5.

14. JP Morgan (1996). *RiskMetrics™-technical document,* 4th ed.
15. Hull, J.C. (2006). Risk Management and Financial Institutions.
16. JP Morgan (1997). *CreditMetrics™-technical document.*
17. Basel Committee on Banking Supervision (February 2003). Sound Practices for the management and Supervision op Operational Risk, Bank for International Settlements.

Chapter 3

The Accounting Perspective

Describes the 2004 COSO framework
  Describes the ERM cube, to include the series of activities
  involved
Gives an example of risk event categorization
Discusses ERM implementation issues

Accounting is responsible for providing stockholders with measures of organizational performance. This includes assurance of accurate financial reporting, which has proven to be fundamental in organizational risk management. Motivated by corporate governance malfeasance exemplified by Enron Corporation, Sarbanes-Oxley placed responsibilities for disclosure and procedures seeking to guarantee honest accounting.

The accounting approach to risk management is centered to a large degree on the standards promulgated by the Committee on Sponsoring Organizations of the Treadway Commission (COSO), generated by the Treadway Commission beginning in 1992. The Sarbanes-Oxley Act of 2002 had a synergistic impact with COSO. While many companies have not used it, COSO offers a framework for organizations to manage risk.[1] Use of COSO was found to be used to a large extent by only 11 percent of the organizations surveyed, and only 15 percent of the respondents believed that their internal auditors used the COSO 1992 framework in full. This finding was supported by a 2005 study conducted by the IIA Research Foundation which found under 12 percent of responding organizations to have complete implementation of ERM, while 14 percent were not going to adopt it.[2] Chief Executive Officers and Chief Financial Officers are required to certify effective internal controls. These controls can be assessed against COSO.[3] This benefits stakeholders. Risk management is now understood to be a strategic activity, and risk standards can ensure uniform risk assessment across the organization. Resources are more likely to be devoted to the most important risk, and better responsiveness to change is obtained.

3.1 The COSO ERM Cube

In 2004, COSO published an *Enterprise Risk Management-Integrated Framework*.[4] The cube considers dimension of objective categories, activities, and organizational levels.

Table 1: COSO ERM Cube

Categories	Activities	Levels
Strategic	Internal Environment	Entity Level
Operations	Objective Setting	Division
Reporting	Event Identification	Business Unit
Compliance	Risk Assessment	Subsidiary
	Risk Response	
	Control Activities	
	Information & Communication	
	Monitoring	

3.1.1 *Categories*

The strategic level involves overarching activities such as organizational governance, strategic objectives, business models, consideration of external forces, and other factors. The operations level is concerned with business processes, value chains, financial flows, and related issues. Reporting includes information systems as well as means to communicate organizational performance on multiple dimensions, to include finance, reputation, and intellectual property. Compliance considers organizational reporting on legal, contractual, and other regulatory requirements (including environmental).

3.1.2 *Activities*

The COSO process consists of a series of actions.[5]

1. **Internal Environment:** The process starts with identification of the organizational units, with <u>entity level</u> representing the overall organization. This includes actions to develop a risk management philosophy, create a risk management culture, and design a risk management organizational structure.

2. **Objective Setting:** Each participating <u>division</u>, <u>business unit</u>, and <u>subsidiary</u> would then identify business objectives and strategic alternatives, reflecting vision for enterprise success. These objectives would be categorized as strategic, operations, reporting, and compliance. These objectives need to be integrated with enterprise objectives at the entity level. Objectives should be clear and strategic, and should reflect the entity-wide risk appetite.

3. **Event Identification:** Management needs to identify events that could influence organizational performance, either positively or negatively. Risk events are identified, along with event interdependencies. (Some events are isolated, while others are correlated.) Measurement issues associated with methodologies or risk assessment techniques need to be considered. O'Donnell (2004) provided a systems view to create a map of the organization's value chain and a taxonomy of categories to identify events that might threaten business performance.[6]

4. **Risk Assessment:** Each of the risks identified in Step 3 are assessed in terms of probability of occurrence, as well as the impact each risk will have on the organization. Thus both impact and likelihood are considered. Their product provides a metric for ranking risks. Assessment techniques can include point estimates, ranges, or best/worst-case scenarios.

5. **Risk Response:** Strategies available to manage risks are developed. These can include risk acceptance, risk avoidance, risk sharing, or risk reduction. Options have been summarized into the four Ts:

    a. **Treating a risk:** taking direct action to reduce impact or likelihood

    b. **Terminate a risk:** discontinue activity exposing the organization to the risk

    c. **Transfer a risk:** insurance or contracts

    d. **Take (or tolerate) a risk:** for areas of organizational expertise, they may decide to accept risk with the idea that they are expert at dealing with it.

Another view considers risk avoidance, reduction, acceptance, transfer, or seeking risks fitting the organization's risk appetite.[7] This is compatible with the four Ts. Avoidance is akin to terminating, acceptance to treating, reduction and transfer to transfer above, and seeking risks to toleration. Risks are necessary to lead to situations likely to offer profit, but risks should be taken only after informed business analysis.

    The effects of risk response on other risks should be considered.

6. **Control Activities:** Controls needed to mitigate identified risks are selected. Implicit in this step is assessment of the costs of each risk response available, and consideration of activities to reduce risks.

7. **Information & Communication:** Control and other risk response activities are put in place to ensure appropriate action is taken within the organization. Organizations need to ensure that information systems can measure and report risk accurately. ERM effectiveness and cost should be communicated to stakeholders.

8. **Monitoring:** As part of an ongoing process, the effectiveness of plan implementation is monitored, feeding back to the control step if problems are encountered. Monitoring includes risk evaluations comparing actual event occurrences with prior estimates of probability, frequency, and cost.

3.2 Event Identification

As an example of how step 3 above can be implemented, Table 2 provides a categorization of risks for financial institutions.

Table 2: Financial Institution Enterprise Risk Management Model[8]

	Top Level	Internal		Specific Risks
External				Regulatory / legal Investor relations Competitors Financial markets Catastrophic loss Sovereign / political issues
	Strategic			Corporate governance Leadership Alignment Planning Communication
	Legal			Compliance Litigation Contractual / obligations Fiduciary
	Reputation			Fraud Ethics Privacy
		Credit		Domestic Foreign
		Market		Valuation Foreign exchange
		Interest Rate Risk		Repricing Yield curve Basis Options
			Operational	Accounting Performance measurement Product development, pricing Business interruption Technology Budgeting & planning Human resources Policy / procedure compliance Customer loyalty / retention

3.2.1 *Risk appetite*

Risks are necessary to do business. Every organization can be viewed as a specialist at dealing with at least one type of risk. Insurance companies specialize in assessing the market value of risks, and offer policies that transfer special types of risks to themselves from their clients at a fee. Banks specialize in the risk of loan repayment, and survive when they are effective at managing these risks. Construction companies specialize in the risks of making buildings or other facilities. However, risks come at organizations from every direction. Those risks that are outside of an organization's specialty are outside that organization's risk appetite. Management needs to assess risks associated with the opportunities it is presented, and accept those that fit their risk appetite (or organizational expertise), and offload other risks in some way (see Step 6 above).

3.3 Example of Risk Quantification

Matyjewicz and D'Arcangelo gave simple examples of how risk assessment could be applied. First, a matrix of risk level (high or low) and control strength (weak or strong) could be generated for each identified risk. Risk impact could be further categorized as critical, significant, moderate, low, or insignificant, while risk probability could have categories of highly probable, probable, likely, unlikely, or remote.

The likely actions of internal auditing were identified. Those risks involving high risk and strong controls would call for checking that inherent risks were in fact mitigated by risk response strategies and controls. Risks involving high risk and weak controls would call for checking for adequacy of management's action plan to improve controls. Those risks assessed as low call for internal auditing to review accuracy of managerial impact evaluation and risk event likelihood.

3.4 Implementation Issues

Past risk management efforts have been characterized by bottom-up implementation.[9] Effective implementation calls for top-down management, as do most organizational efforts. Without top support, lack of funding will starve most efforts. Related to that, top support is needed to coordinate efforts so that silo mentalities don't take over. COSO requires a holistic approach. If COSO is adopted within daily processes, it can effectively strengthen corporate governance. Another important issue is the application of sufficient resources to effectively implement ERM.

One view of ERM, parallel to that of the CMI system used in software engineering, is as follows.[10]

1. Level 1: **Compliance** – review of policy and procedure with a checklist orientation, providing low value to the organization in terms of ERM.
2. Level 2: **Control** – implementation of control frameworks, still using a checklist orientation, also providing low value to organizations.
3. Level 3: **Process** – taking a process view across departments, focusing on effectiveness as well as efficiency, to include process mapping.
4. Level 4: **Risk Management** – use of shared risk language, with the ability to prioritize efforts based on process mapping.
5. Level 5: **Enterprise Risk Management** – the Nirvana of holistic risk reviews tied to entity strategy based on common risk language, viewing risk management as a process, providing high value to organizational risk management.

3.5 Conclusions

Gupta and Thomson identified problems in implementing COSO.[11] Small companies (fewer than 1000 employees) reported a less favorable impression of COSO. Complaints in general included vagueness and nonspecificity for auditing. COSO was viewed as high-level, and thus open to interpretation at the operational level. This seems to reflect a view by most organizations reflective of Level 1 and Level 2 in Bowling and Rieger's framework. Other complaints about COSO have been published.[12] One is that the 1992 framework is not completely appropriate for 2006.[13] The subsequent COSO ERM is more current, but some view it as vague, simplistic, and provides little implementation guidance.

A number of specific approaches for various steps have been published. Later studies have indicated about one half of the surveyed organizations to have either adopted or were in the process of implementing ERM, indicating some increase.[14] Carnaghan reviewed procedures for business process modeling.[15] If such approaches are utilized, more effective ERM can be obtained through COSO.

Endnotes

1. Gupta, P.P., Thomson, J.C. (2006). Use of COSO 1992 in management reporting on internal control, *Strategic Finance* 88:3, 27-33.
2. Gramling, A.A., Myers, P.M. (2006). Internal auditing's role in ERM, *Internal Auditor* 63:2, 52-58.
3. Matyjewicz, G., D'Arcangelo, J.R. (2004). Beyond Sarbanes-Oxley, *Internal Auditor* 61:5, 67-72.
4. Matyjewicz & D'Arcangelo (2004), op. cit.; Ballou, B., Heitger, D.L. (2005). A building-block approach for implementing COSO's enterprise risk management-integrated framework, *Management Accounting Quarterly* 6:2, 1-10.
5. Balou & Heitzer (2005), op cit.
6. O'Donnell, E. (2005). Enterprise risk management: A systems-thinking framework for the event identification phase, *International Journal of Accounting Information Systems* 6:3, 177-195.
7. Drew, M. (2007). Information risk management and compliance – Expect the unexpected, *BT Technology Journal* 25:1, 19-29.
8. Bowling, B.M., Rieger, L. (2005b). Success factors for implementing enterprise risk management, *Bank Accounting and Finance* 18:3, 21-26.
9. Extracted and modified from Bowling, D.M., Rieger, L.A. (2005a). Making sense of COSO's new framework for enterprise risk management, *Bank Accounting and Finance* 18:2, 29-34.
10. Bowling & Rieger 2005b, op cit.

11. Gupta & Thomson (2004), op. cit.
12. Quinn, L.R. (2006). COSO at a crossroad, *Strategic Finance* 88:1, 42-49.
13. Ibid.
14. Gramling, A.A., Myers, P.M. (2006), op cit.
15. Carnaghan, C. (2006). Business process modeling approaches in the context of process level audit risk assessment: An analysis and comparison, *International Journal of Accounting Information Systems* 7:2, 170-204.

Chapter 4

Supply Chain Risk Management

Reviews the benefits of supply chains in marketing products to
  customers
Considers reduction of risks in supply chains
Discusses issues in supply chain management
Discusses the risks involved in supply chain disruption

The Internet allows business to be conducted all over the globe. This presents many new opportunities for organizations to market to new customers, and thus improve their business opportunities.

It is interesting to compare the old way of organizing business by vertical integration, made so successful by John D. Rockefeller and Standard Oil, by U.S. Steel, Alcoa, and others. They took the idea of system logistics developed by the military and applied it to business, taking the approach that if there was any profit to be made in their supply chain, they wanted it. This led to vertical supply chains connecting mines, processing, transportation, and various forms of production to different levels of marketing for massive monopolies. Enforcement of such monopolies was easiest in businesses calling for high capital investment.

The modern way of conducting business is quite different. The formerly adversarial relationships of 19th and early 20th Century business have been replaced by cooperative arrangements of supply chain members. The focus is on being more competitive, and thus emphasizing services related to the products being made. There also is an emphasis on linking together specialists, with a dynamic integration of often reasonably independent entities to work together to deliver

45

goods and services. Goods and services seem ever less distinguishable, making the old dichotomy of operations passé.

Global competition, technological change, and continual search for competitive advantage have motivated risk management in supply chains.[1] Supply chains are often complex systems of networks, reaching hundreds or thousands of participants from around the globe in some cases (Wal-Mart or Dell). The term has been used both at the strategic level (coordination and collaboration) and tactical level (management of logistics across functions and between businesses).[2] In this sense, risk management can focus on identification of better ways and means of accomplishing organizational objectives rather than simply preservation of assets or risk avoidance. Supply chain risk management is interested in coordination and collaboration of processes and activities across functions within a network of organizations. Tang provided a framework of risk management perspectives in supply chains.[3] Supply chains enable manufacturing outsourcing to take advantages of global relative advantages, as well as increase product variety. There are many risks inherent in this more open, dynamic system.

4.1 Supply Chain Risk Management Process

Tang reviewed four risk reduction strategies used within supply chains:[4]

1. Identification of different types of risk,
2. Estimation of likelihood of each event;
3. Assessment of potential loss from major disruption,
4. Identification of strategies to reduce risk.

Because data is often scarce, especially for new experiences, estimation of likelihoods can be an issue. Most companies were found to use of a range of assessment programs, from formal quantitative models to informal qualitative plans, There has been increased contingency planning to meet legal requirements from the Sarbanes-Oxley Act of 2002 in the U.S., or KonTraG of 1998 in Germany. A simple means to reduce risk is the use of multiple suppliers for critical materials.

The U.S. defense industry adopts the Supply Chain Risk Management approach consisting of the following stages:[5]

1. Risk planning – consideration for assessing, handling, and communicating supply chain risks for a program, to include establishment of risk priorities, training, and responsibility of various stakeholders.
2. Risk identification – discovery and documentation of supply chain risks.
3. Risk analysis – assessment of each risk by likelihood of occurrence over the life of the program, and estimated impact measured in terms of delivery, cost, and quality.
4. Risk handling – stakeholders rank-order risks and identify options for mitigation of the most likely and most serious. Mitigation can aim at lowering likelihood or impact.
5. Risk monitoring – risks are tracked for occurrence, as well as for the effectiveness of risk handling plans in terms of cost, schedule, and performance.

Another view of a supply chain risk management process includes steps for risk identification, risk assessment, risk avoidance, and risk mitigation.[6] These structures for handling risk are compatible with Tang's list given above, but focus on the broader aspects of the process.

4.1.1 *Risk identification*

Risks in supply chains can include operational risks and disruptions. Operational risks involve inherent uncertainties for supply chain elements such as customer demand, supply, and cost. Disruption risks come from disasters (natural in the form of floods, hurricanes, etc.; man-made in the form of terrorist attacks or wars) and from economic crises (currency reevaluations, strikes, shifting market prices). Most quantitative analyses and methods are focused on operational risks. Disruptions are more dramatic, less predictable, and thus are much more difficult to model. Risk management planning and response for disruption are usually qualitative.

4.1.2 *Risk assessment*

Theoretically, risk has been viewed as applying to those cases where odds are known, and uncertainty to those cases where odds are not known. Risk is a preferable basis for decision making, but life often presents decision makers with cases of uncertainty. The issue is further complicated in that perfectly rational decision makers may have radically different approaches to risk. Qualitative risk management depends a great deal on managerial attitude towards risk. Different rational individuals are likely to have different response to risk avoidance, which usually is inversely related to return, thus leading to a tradeoff decision. Research into cognitive psychology has found that managers are often insensitive to probability estimates of possible outcomes, and tend to ignore possible events that they consider to be unlikely.[7] Furthermore, managers tend to pay little attention to uncertainty involved with positive outcomes.[8] They tend to focus on critical performance targets, which makes their response to risk contingent upon context.[9] Some approaches to theoretical decision making prefer objective treatment of risk through quantitative scientific measures following normative ideas of how humans should make decisions. Business involves an untheoretical construct, however, with high levels of uncertainty (data not available) and consideration of multiple (often conflicting) factors, making qualitative approaches based upon perceived managerial risk more appropriate.

Because accurate measures of factors such as probability are often lacking, robust strategies (more likely to enable effective response under a wide range of circumstances) are often attractive to risk managers. Strategies are efficient if they enable a firm to deal with operational risks efficiently regardless of major disruptions. Strategies are resilient if they enable a firm to keep operating despite major disruptions. Supply chain risk can arise from many sources, including the following:[10]

- Political events
- Product availability
- Distance from source
- Industry capacity

- Demand fluctuation
- Changes in technology
- Changes in labor markets
- Financial instability
- Management turnover.

4.1.3 *Risk avoidance*

The oldest form of risk avoidance is probably insurance, purchasing some level of financial security from an underwriter. This focuses on the financial aspects of risk, and is reactive, providing some recovery after a negative experience. Insurance is not the only form of risk management used in supply chains. Delta Airlines insurance premiums for terrorism increased from $2 million in 2001 to $152 million in 2002.[11] Insurance focuses on financial risks. Other major risks include loss of customers due to supply change disruption.

Supply chain risks can be buffered by a variety of methods. Purchasing is usually assigned the responsibility of controlling costs and assuring continuity of supply. Buffers in the form of inventories exist to provide some risk reduction, at a cost of higher inventory holding cost. Giunipero and Al Eltantawy compared traditional practices with newer risk management approaches.[12] The traditional practice, relying upon extra inventory, multiple suppliers, expediting, and frequent supplier changes suffered from high transaction costs, long purchase fulfillment cycle times, and expensive rush orders. Risk management approaches, drawing upon practices such as supply chain alliances, e-procurement, just-in-time delivery, increased coordination and other techniques, provides more visibility in supply chain operations. There may be higher prices incurred for goods, and increased security issues, but methods have been developed to provide sound electronic business security.

4.1.4 *Risk mitigation*

Tang provided four basic risk mitigation approaches for supply chains.[13] These focus on the sources of risk: management of uncertainty with respect to supply, to demand, to product management, and information management. Furthermore, there are both strategic and tactical aspects involved. Strategically, network design can enable better control of supply risks. Strategies such as product pricing and rollovers can control demand to a degree. Greater product variety can strategically protect against product risks. And systems providing greater information visibility across supply chain members can enable better coping with risks. Tactical decisions include supplier selection and order allocation (including contractual arrangements); demand control over time, markets, and products; product promotion; and information sharing, vendor managed inventory systems, and collaborative planning, forecasting, and replenishment.

4.2 Supply Management

Cost advantages are available to supply chain core organizations from outsourcing non-core functions.[14] There are five interrelated issues in supply management:[15]

1. Supply network design
2. Supplier relationships
3. Supplier selection process
4. Supplier order allocation
5. Supply contracts

Design of an effective supply chain network needs to configure the network (link suppliers, manufacturing facilities, distribution centers, warehouses, etc.), assign products to facilities, assign customers to appropriate facilities, and to plan how much and when each facility is to produce and ship.

A variety of supplier relationships are possible, varying the degree of linkage between vendor and core organizations. Different types of contracts and information exchange are possible, and different schemes for pricing and coordinating schedules.

4.2.1 *Supplier selection process*

Supplier (vendor) evaluation is a very important operational decision. There are decisions selecting which suppliers to employ, as well as decisions with respect to quantities to order from each supplier. With the increase in outsourcing and the opportunities provided by electronic business to tap world-wide markets, these decisions are becoming ever more complex. The presence of multiple criteria in these decisions has long been recognized.[16] A probabilistic model for this decision has been published to include the following criteria:[17]

1. Quality personnel
2. Quality procedure
3. Concern for quality
4. Company history
5. Price relative to quality
6. Actual price
7. Financial ability
8. Technical performance
9. Delivery history
10. Technical assistance
11. Production capability
12. Manufacturing equipment

Some of these criteria overlap, and other criteria may exist for specific supply chain decision makers. But clearly there are many important aspects to selecting suppliers.

4.2.2 *Supplier order allocation*

Operational risks in supply chain order allocation include uncertainties in demands, supply yields, lead times, and costs. Thus not only do specific suppliers need to be selected, the quantities purchased from them needs to be determined on a recurring basis.

Supply chains provide many valuable benefits to their members, but also create problems of coordination that manifest themselves in the "bullwhip" effect.[18] Information system coordination can reduce some of the negative manifestations of the bullwhip effect, but there still remains the issue of profit sharing. Decisions that are optimal for one supply chain member often have negative impacts of the total profitability of the entire supply chain.[19]

4.3 Demand Management

Demand management approaches include using statistics in models for identification of an optimal portfolio of demand distributions[20] and economic models to select strategies using price as a response mechanism to change demand.[21]   Other strategies include shifting demand over time, across markets, or across products.   Demand management of course is one of the aims of advertising and other promotional activities. However, it has long been noted as one of the most difficult things to predict over time.

4.4 Product Management

An effective strategy to manage product risk is variety, which can be used to increase market share to serve distinct segments of a market. The basic idea is to diversify products to meet the specific needs of each market segment. However, while this would be expected to increase revenues and market share, it will lead to increase manufacturing costs and inventory costs.

Various ways to deal with the potential inefficiencies in product variety include Dell's make-to-order strategy.

4.5 Information Management

E-business has brought us an entirely new business climate, with the ability to electronically generate retail data. Many service organizations and retail outlets generate masses of data. Grocery stores have large amounts of data generated by their purchases. Bar coding has made checkout very convenient for retail establishments. Wal-Mart and other retailers have extended electronic data generation to include radio frequency identification (RFID), allowing tracking of product physical location in real time. The electronic age involves data on a very large scale.

Successful retail organizations in the 21st Century consider service to the customer to be their focal point. IT systems applied across supply chains are enablers so that retail organizations can provide better service. Supply chains involve major risks. There have been a variety of control schemas that have evolved to control supply networks. The traditional uncoordinated supply chains of the 1980s, with no information sharing, but independent inventory control policies, led to the infamous "bullwhip" phenomenon.[22] The bullwhip phenomenon occurs because of overestimation of demand induced by the lumpiness of orders from downstream elements of the supply chain. An obvious first step in reducing the inefficiencies caused by the bullwhip effect was to increase information sharing across the supply chain.[23] The use of bounded ordering policies has been suggested as an additional means to reduce bullwhip effect.[24] In a short season environment, the benefits of improved forecasting and production planning have been suggested.[25] More complete information sharing and coordination systems have also been studied.[26]

4.5.1 *Traditional supply chains*

The first type of coordination among supply chain members to alleviate bullwhip risk is information exchange (**efficient consumer response**), to include action plans to enable forecast alignment for long-term and capacity planning.[27] This improves visibility and thus makes demand more predictable. Faster transfer of information across organizations has not avoided all difficulties.[28] Problems have included slow item level replenishment as opposed to fast order placement. Retailers in the grocery industry carry tens of thousands (if not hundreds of thousands) of specific stock-keeping units. In this complex environment, an order may be placed after product is sold. Furthermore, small items are often delivered in bulk packages, which can lead to difficulties. On the supplier side, short lead-time and high service level requirements squeeze out most reaction time. If extremely accurate information at a detailed level is not available, the system almost guarantees stock-outs. Avoiding such stock-outs through higher inventories in turn eliminates most of the benefits of a well-managed inventory system.

Vendor managed inventory (VMI) involves supplier assumption of management of retailer inventory. This is channel coordination. Based upon advanced information through electronic data interchange (EDI) or Internet, the supplier controls the stock at the retailer. VMI has been analytically shown to yield superior performance over traditional supply chain systems.[29] VMI would optimize the overall profits of the supply chain, as it is superior to traditional local inventory management.[30] VMI can gain efficiencies through shipment consolidation.[31] VMI allows retailers to expand the assortment of products they carried in a given retail space, thus improving brand profitability for both retailer and vendor.

VMI has been adopted by many firms. However, problems have been experienced, and has been abandoned in some cases.[32] VMI's major weakness to be insufficient visibility over the entire supply chain in some cases.[33] VMI was found to work well when manufacturers supplied large volumes of frequently replenished products under relatively stable sales conditions. But high levels of demand volatility were found to lead to excessive inventories, the same problem that existed in traditional retail inventory control through the bullwhip effect. VMI has been found to perform better when manufacturer effort was a substantial driver of consumer demand, and when consumers were unlikely to purchase substitutes in cases of stock-out. But when substitution was attractive, VMI could lead to poorer performance than traditional retailer managed inventory.[34]

Continuous replenishment (CR) was proposed to implement automatic replenishment programs, where sellers restocked retailer inventory based upon actual product usage and stock level information provided by the retailer. Wal-Mart piloted CR in 1995, and it has been used by larger US and UK retailers. Retailers made point-of-sales data available to suppliers, making it possible to base inventory decisions on sales forecasts rather than inventory level variations. CR enhanced VMI by requiring supply chain members to share more information and data, and to utilize common systems and use common performance measures.

This promoted joint decision-making, accountability, and incentives for performance. CR has been cited as successful in improving customer service levels, and in improving inventory turnover.[35] However, because CR does not necessarily cover inventories throughout the supply chain, it still can include gaps. Manufacturer prediction of future retail events is the major missing feature of CR. Excess inventory seems to be shifted from retailers and distributors to manufacturers. While CR improved VMI, further benefits were available.

4.5.2 *Collaborative planning, forecasting and replenishment*

Collaborative planning, forecasting and replenishment (CPFR) was the next step, applied in the drug, grocery, apparel, and other industries.[36] The manufacturer and retail exchange marketplace information to develop customer-specific plans to substantially reduce inventory. Promotion schedules, point-of-sale data, and inventory data are shared to enable shortening lead-times and integration of forecasting and replenishment. Thus total visibility is obtained, and changing demand patterns can be considered.

The way in which information is exchanged early yields a number of benefits.[37] For retailers, these include increased sales, faster response times to orders, higher service levels despite lower inventories which in turn lead to lower costs from obsolescence and deterioration. Manufacturers benefit through increased sales, higher fill rates for orders, faster cycle times, lower capacity requirements, and lower product inventories. There are fewer stocking points needed over the supply chain, there is improved forecast accuracy, and overall, lower expenses over the system.

Micheau described the implementation of a system by Boeing and Alcoa that includes the features of CPFR.[38] The problem in that case, involving Alcoa supplying aluminum products for Boeing airplanes, included rail transportation which involved unreliable delivery dates. The presence of minimum quantities in multiple bundles distorted forecasts. The two companies planned several supply chain elements to overcome difficulties. Information systems were integrated, allowing real-time information exchange. Operations were tightly linked between supplier and manufacturer. Lean manufacturing principles were applied. Close cooperation led to an atmosphere with high levels of trust. Boeing sent weekly electronic forecasts and inventory counts to Alcoa, and used its ERP system to generate electronic purchase orders for raw materials. Alcoa implemented a vendor-managed inventory system, and improved forecast visibility in their system. Alcoa also had to change its order entry process to accept Boeing orders. The electronic forecasting system was credited with expediting information exchange. Boeing carefully checked its forecasting, and identified modifications to data obtained from their ERP system that were needed to provide Alcoa with more accurate data. The greater degree of forecasting accuracy obtained enabled Alcoa to make more efficient production decisions. A blanket purchase order for a year was used to override the ERP generated purchasing system. Forecasts were aggregated by week.

CPFR has encountered some barriers. As with VMI, systems need to be compatible across organizations, and the more organizations involved, the more restrictive this requirement is.

4.5.3 *E-commerce security*

E-procurement has provided significant cost reduction to supply chain alliance partners. Transaction costs have been estimated to be $40 to $400 for sales representatives, $2 to $5 for telephone contacts, but only $0.10 to $0.40 via Internet.[39] Bid solicitation can be accomplished through electronic reverse auctions, providing buyers with a package of goods from many sellers competing in online auctions. There are risks from hackers or competitors gaining proprietarial information over the Web. Counterfeit products can be introduced into systems, both in e-commerce or otherwise. Johnson & Johnson found that face surgical mesh was being distributed to surgeons in 2003. They hired Ernst & Young LLP to investigate, finding widespread counterfeiting.[40] In the global prescription drug industry, a cough syrup originating from China was found to be poisoning users in a number of customer countries throughout the world.[41] However, electronic security is available through e-business systems. A bigger risk comes from focusing solely on price. This creates some additional risk (service, quality, and delivery may also be important), large cost savings have been attained through on-line auctions.

E-commerce security risks can be reduced by better hiring or training of employees, or through certification and auditing of outsourcing partners. Long-term alliances also lead to reduced risks.

4.6 Supply Chain Disruption

Tang classified supply chain vulnerabilities as those due to uncertain economic cycles, customer demand, and disasters. Land Rover reduced their workforce by over one thousand when a key supplier went insolvent. Dole was affected by Hurricane Mitch hitting their banana plantations in Central America in 1998. September 11, 2001 suspended air traffic, leading Ford Motor Company to close five plants for several days.[42] Many things can disrupt supply chains. Supply chain disruptions have been found to negatively impact stock returns for firms suffering them.[43]

4.6.1 *Examples of supply chain resilience* [44]

The Indonesian Rupiah was devalued over 50 percent in 1997, causing severe problems for Indonesian suppliers to pay for imported components or materials, blocking their participation in supply chains serving the U.S. Jakarta's public transport system reduced operations due to high prices for bus repair parts. The automobile manufacturer Astra suspended production due to the price of imported parts. Many chemical plants halted production due to the cost of imported raw materials. Many U.S. manufacturers had outsourcing arrangements with Indonesian firms. Li and Fung, a Hong Kong trading company in durable goods to include textiles, shifted production from Indonesia to other Asian sources, and provided lines of credit and loans to their Indonesian suppliers. This enabled on-time fulfillment of orders to U.S. customers, and enhanced Li and Fung's reputation, playing a role in their sales growth.

An earthquake hit Taiwan in 1999. Several Taiwanese members of Dell and Apple supply chains were unable to deliver computer components for a few weeks. Apple experienced shortages for components needed to produce iBook and G4 computers, and tried to use a slower version of G4 computers to fill current orders. This led to customer complaints. Conversely, Dell customers did not notice the component shortage, as Dell offered special price incentives to encourage online customers to purchase computer systems using alternative components.

In March 2000, a Philips semiconductor plant in New Mexico, a key supplier of cellular telephone radio frequency chips, burnt. Two European telephone manufacturers adopted different response strategies with starkly contrasting results. Ericsson reacted slowly, losing sales revenue of about 400 Euros. Nokia had designed their mobile phones using modular components and obtained multiple sources of chips. Nokia had to reconfigure their design slightly, but were able to smoothly satisfy customer demand and actually strengthen their market position.[45]

4.6.2 *Robust strategies*

Tang gave nine robust supply chain strategies that have proven useful in coping with supply chain disruption.

1. **Postponement** relies on design concepts to include standardization, commonality, and modular design to delay the point of product differentiation. A more generic product is produced based on aggregate demand, applying customization to specific products later in the production cycle. This enables a more flexible response to specific product demands. Nokia's response to the Philips fire in 2000 was an example of this strategy, which has also been used by Xilinx (producer of programmable logic chips), Hewlett-Packard (who utilized postponement by mass-producing a generic workstation using production to stock), and Benneton (who produced undyed sweaters, later dyed as needed by customer orders). Postponement

improves the ability to manage supplies and accomplishes greater product flexibility.

2. **Strategic stock** is used to gain the benefits of safety stock for key items without the excessive expense incurred in excessive inventories for all items. Examples include Toyota, who inventoried cars at key distribution locations to assure ample supply in particular regions, and by Sears doing the same thing with appliances. This allows higher customer service levels without excessive inventory holding costs. Similar strategies are used by the Center for Disease Control in medical supplies. Strategic stocks increase product availability, enabling quicker response.

3. **Flexible supply base** strategy mitigates risks from sole sourcing through multiple suppliers. Hewlett-Packard used plants in Washington state and in Singapore for inkjet printers, relying upon the less expensive Singapore plant for base volume, and the Washington plant to satisfy demand fluctuations. This enabled some volume slack to cope with supply disruption through increasing supply flexibility.

4. **Make-and-buy** strategy is the same idea as flexible supply base, only including external production as an alternative source. Hewlett-Packard again used this strategy for DeskJet printers, which were primarily outsourced to a Malaysian manufacturer, with the Singapore factory handling a portion of their production. Zara is famous for applying this principle in fashion clothing. Benefits are the same as with a flexible supply base.

5. **Economic supply incentives** can be used even if production cannot be shifted. The U.S. market supply for flu vaccine of a specific type was reduced due to uncertain demand and governmental price pressure. That left two vaccine producers in the U.S. In October 2005, one of these was suspended due to identification of bacteria contamination, leading to an expected shortage of 48 million flue shots, and subsequent rationing to high-risk groups. Use of economic supply incentives could increase participation in this market, averting future shortages. In a similar example, Intercon Japan had one key supplier, and

became concerned about the supplier's monopoly position. Intercon Japan offered economic incentives to Nagoya Steel to develop a new steel process to produce their cable connectors, including minimum order quantities, technical advice, and market demand information. This enabled Intercon Japan to keep price pressure on its original supplier, attaining increased product availability and enabling them to be able to quickly adjust order quantities.

6. **Flexible transportation** is a strategy provides assurance of delivery. It can be accomplished in a variety of ways, to include multi-modal transportation. Seven-Eleven Japan encouraged its logistics partner to diversity into a system of trucks, motorcycles, bicycles, ships, and helicopters. This enabled Seven-Eleven Japan to rush delivery of rice balls to Kobe earthquake victims in the later 1980s. Multi-carrier transportation ensures continuous flow of materials. Alliances of cargo airlines have been able to quickly switch carriers when faced with regional political disruptions, and also allows lower-cost delivery. Use of multiple routes is a third transportation strategy enabling bypassing temporary bottlenecks. When US west coast ports were shut down in 2002, shipments from Asia could use the Panama Canal to reach east coast ports.

7. **Dynamic pricing and promotion** are forms of revenue management strategies. Airline yield management systems are a manifestation of this strategy, providing gains of almost $1 billion for American Airlines.[46] Dell also applied low-cost upgrade options to customers when faced with supply disruptions from the Taiwanese earthquake in 1999 mentioned earlier. Revenue management increases control over product demand, enabling the firm to influence customer product selection.

8. **Dynamic assortment planning** is a strategy based on influencing consumer product demand by display location. Supermarkets manipulate demand on a routine basis through product positioning. This again increases control of product demand.

9. **Silent product rollover** involves slow leaking of new products
   without formal announcement. This encourages customers to
   select available products instead of asking for products that have
   been phased out or that are out of stock. Examples of this
   strategy are Swatch, which produces each product once, or Zara,
   which launches new fashion collections without fanfare. All
   products are thus substitutes, which expedites dealing with
   demand fluctuations as well as coping with supply or demand
   disruption.

Any strategy will have downsides. The costs and benefits in each
specific case are often difficult to quantify, especially due to the factor
of competitiveness. Each organization needs to consider its overall
business strategy. Firms that desire to focus on a limited number of
products for strategic reasons will find little value in the postponement
strategy. Wal-Mart strategically emphasizes a low-cost strategy, and
thus dynamic pricing and promotion make little sense for their situation.
Strategies also need to be feasible. During the 2002 longshoreman's
strike on the U.S. west coast, a Toyota-General Motors venture relied
upon a 6-day inventory to deal with disruptions. However, the strike
turned out to last longer than that period, making it impossible to unload
components sitting in west coast ports for rerouting.

4.7 Conclusions

Supply chains have become important elements in the conduct of global
business. There are too many efficiency factors available from global
linkages to avoid. We all gain from allowing broader participation by
those with relative advantages. Alliances can serve as safety nets by
providing alternative sources, routes, or products for its members. Risk
exposure within supply chains can be reduced by reducing lead times. A
common means of accomplishing lead time reduction is by collocation of
suppliers at producer facilities.

This chapter has discussed some of the many risks associated with
supply chains. A rational process of dealing with these risks includes
assessment of what can go wrong, quantitative measurement to the

degree possible of risk likelihood and severity, qualitative planning to cover a broader set of important criteria, and contingency planning. A wide variety of available supply chain risk-reduction strategies were reviewed, with cases of real application.

While no supply chain network can expect to anticipate all future disruptions, they can set in place a process to reduce exposure and impact. Preplanned response is expected to provide better organizational response in keeping with organizational objectives.

Endnotes

1. Ritchie, B., Brindly, C. (2007). Supply chain risk management and performance: A guiding framework for future development, *International Journal of Operations & Production Management* 27:3, 303-322.
2. Mentzer, J.T., Dewitt, W., Keebler, J.S., Min, S., Nix, N.W., Smith, C.D., Zacharia, Z.G. (2001). *Supply Chain Management*. Thousand Oaks, CA: Sage.
3. Tang, C.S. (2006a). Perspectives in supply chain risk management, *International Journal of Production Economics* 103, 451-488.
4. Tang, C.S. (2006b). Robust strategies for mitigating supply chain disruptions, *International Journal of Logistics: Research and Applications* 9:1, 33-45.
5. VanderBok, R., Sauter, J.A., Bryan, C., Horan, J. (2007). Manage your supply chain risk, *Manufacturing Engineering* 138:3, 153-153-156, 158, 160-161.
6. Chapman, P., Cristopher, M., Juttner, U., Peck, H., Wilding, R. (2002). Identification and managing supply chain vulnerability, *Logistics and Transportation Focus* 4:4, 59-64.
7. Kunreuther, H. (1976). Limited knowledge and insurance protection, *Public Policy* 24, 227-261.
8. MacCrimmon, K.R., Wehrung, D.A. (1986). *Taking Risks: The Management of Uncertainty*. New York: Free Press.
9. March, J., Shapira, Z. (1987). Managerial perspectives on risk and risk taking, *Management Science* 33, 1404-1418.

10. Giunipero, L.C., Aly Eltantawy, R. (2004). Securing the upstream supply chain: A risk management approach, *International Journal of Physical Distribution & Logistics Management* 34:9, 698-713.
11. Rice, B., Caniato, F. (2003). Supply chain response to terrorism: Creating resilient and secure supply chains, *Supply Chain Response to Terrorism Project Interim Report*. Cambridge, MA: MIT Center for Transportation and Logistics.
12. Giunipero and Aly Eltantawy (2004), op cit.
13. Tang (2006a), op cit.
14. Porter, M. (1985). *Competitive Advantage*. New York: The Free Press.
15. Tang (2006a), op cit.
16. Dickson, G.W. (1966). An analysis of vendor selection systems and decisions, *Journal of Purchasing* 2, 5-17.
17. Moskowitz, H., Tang, J., Lam, P. (2000). Distribution of aggregate utility using stochastic elements of additive multiattribute utility models, *Decision Sciences* 31, 327-360.
18. Sterman, J.D. (1989). Modeling managerial behavior: Misperceptions of feedback in a dynamic decision making experiment, *Management Science* 35, 321-339.
19. Bresnahan, T.F., Reiss, P.C. (1985). Dealer and manufacturer margins, *Rand Journal of Economics* 16, 253-268.
20. Carr, S., Lovejoy, W. (2000). The inverse newsvendor problem: Choosing an optimal demand portfolio for capacitated resources, *Management Science* 47, 912-927.
21. Van Mieghem, J., Dada, M. (2001). Price versus production postponement: Capacity and competition, *Management Science* 45, 1631-1649.
22. Sterman, J.D. (1989). Modeling managerial behavior: misperceptions of feedback in a dynamic decision making experiment, *Management Science* 35:3, 321-339.
23. Hariharan, R., and Zipkin, P. (1995). Customer-order information, lead-times, and inventories, *Management Science*, 41:10, 1599-1607.
24. Gavirneni, S., Kapuscinski, R., and Tayur, S. (1999). Value of information in capacitated supply chains. *Management Science*, 45:1, 16-24.

25. Fisher, M., and Raman, A. (1996). Reducing the cost of demand uncertainty through accurate response to early sales, *Operations Research*, 44:1, 87-99.
26. Cachon, G., Fisher, M. (2000). Supply chain inventory management and the value of shared information. *Management Science*, 46:8, 1032-1048; Chen, F., Federgruen, A., Zheng, Y.S. (2001). Coordination Mechanisms For A Distribution System With One Supplier and Multiple Retailers. *Management Science*, 47:5, 693-708.
27. Holweg, M., Disney, S., Holström, J., Småros, J. (2005). Supply chain collaboration: making sense of the strategy continuum. *European Management Journal*, 23:2, 170-181.
28. Kaipia, R., Holmström, J., Tanskanen, K. (2002). VMI: What are you losing if you let your customer place orders? *Production Planning & Control*, 13:1, 17-25.
29. Waller, M., Johnson, J.E., Davis, T. (1999). Vendor-Managed Inventory in the retail supply chain, *Journal of Business Logistics*, 20:1, 183-203.
30. Cohen Kulp, S. (2002). The effect of information precision and reliability on manufacturer-retailer relationships. *The Accounting Review* 77:3, 653-677.
31. Cetinkaya, S., Lee, C.Y. (2000). Stock replenishment and shipment scheduling for vendor-managed inventory systems, *Management Science* 46:2, 217-232.
32. Fry, M.J., Kapuscinski, R., Lennon Olsen, T. (2001). Coordinating production and delivery under a (z, Z)-type vendor-managed inventory contract, *Manufacturing & Service Operations Management* 3:2, 151-173.
33. Barratt (2003), op cit.
34. Kraiselburd, S., Narayanan, V.G., Raman, A. (2004). Contracting in a supply chain with stochastic demand and substitute products, *Production and Operations Management* 13:1, 46-62.
35. Vergin, R.C. (1998). An examination of inventory turnover in the fortune 500 industrial companies, *Production and Inventory Management Journal* 39, 51-56.

36. Ireland, R., Bruce, R. (2000). CPFR: only the beginning of collaboration, *Supply Chain Management Review* 4:4, 80-88.
37. Fliedner, G. (2003). CPFR: an emerging supply chain tool, *Industrial Management & Data Systems* 103:1, 14-21.
38. Micheau, V.A. (2005). How Boeing and Alcoa implemented a successful vendor managed inventory program, *The Journal of Business Forecasting*, Spring 17-19.
39. Antonette, G., Giunipero, L.C., Sawchuk, C. (2002). *E-purchasing Plus: Transforming Supply Management Through Technology*. Goshen, NY: JGC Enterprises.
40. Wald, J., Holleran, J. (2007). Counterfeit products and faulty supply chain, *Risk Management* 54:4, 58-62.
41. Wade, J. (2007). The bittersweet poison in the prescription drug supply chain, *Risk Management* 54:7, 12.
42. Tang (2006b), op cit.
43. Hendricks, K., Singhal, V. (2005). An empirical analysis of the effect of supply chain disruptions on long-run stock price performance and equity risk of the firm, *Production and Operations Management* 25-53.
44. Tang (2006b), op cit.
45. Hopkins, K. (2005). Value opportunity three: Improving the ability to fulfill demand, *Business Week* 13 January.
46. Cook, T. (1998). Sabre soars. *OR/MS Today*, June.

Chapter 5

Information Systems Perspective

Considers risks in organizational information systems
Reviews COSO as applied to information system risk management
Presents methods to identify information system risks
Gives a systems view of enterprise systems
Describes enterprise system risk criteria

Technology is developing at a rapid pace, outstripping the rate of growth in population (which we hope is slowing down), the economy (which we hope is increasing at a controlled rate), and culture (which we want to speed up). Every year we see at least one significant advance in computer speed and computer system storage capacity. Every year we purchase a new iPod, expecting it to be outdated in a year. Every year we expect last year's cell phone to be an antique, and that Intel will build a faster chip, leading to a new generation of personal computers.

Information technology makes it possible to radically change how business is done. Globalization has had a major impact (the Internet makes it possible to reach customers worldwide, and to outsource work to producers worldwide). Technologically, once standardization is accomplished through service oriented architecture, it is possible to link software tools from many sources in a dynamic business system. But there are negative developments as well. Flash viruses, worms, distributed denial of service attacks, phishing and other evils have quickly spread.[1] Terror has also become a possibility. Corporate behavior, such as exhibited by Enron and WorldCom, also create a more turbulent information system environment.

This makes long term investment in technology problematic. It is hard to have a rational long-term business plan if the conditions concerning product availability are going to be completely revised. That is one of the factors of life that make the future interesting. We need to learn to keep up with new developments, which lead to new opportunities. It has always been the case that we need to adapt – but now we need to adapt much faster.

This chapter will discuss risk aspects of information systems. Technological developments occur at an ever-increasing pace. System interactions can lead to unintended consequences, which call for us to be prepared for change and to respond to new challenges.

5.1 Information Systems Risk

Risks in information systems can be viewed from four perspectives.[2] **Business disruption** risks come from external sources. Information technology is faced by physical threats (flood, fire, etc.), intrusion (hackers and other malicious invasions), or functional failure (inaccurate data, reporting systems not providing required information to management and/or operations). Physical security is usually dealt with by one group of people, while IT personnel are usually responsible for risks involving intrusion or function. **Relational** risk occur between IT personnel and vendors, third parties, or other parts of the enterprise. This type of risk is more a function of human interaction. **Technology risks** relate to assuring that the system is response to enterprise needs, complying with standards that allow communication within and outside the organization, and that sound information technology maintenance and project management procedures are in place. **IT governance** risks relate to strategy, IT resources, and compliance or legal issues.

Anderson called for converging IT and physical security under the direction of a single strategic leader, allowing focus on organizational business objectives.[3] He suggested focus on each organization's unique characteristics considering company size, industry regulations, liability, technical complexity, culture, and risk tolerance. Convergence of physical and IT security are expected to align security efforts with business objectives and allow better risk focus. It also can lead to reduced overhead and administrative duplication. Interaction of system components can lead to better detection of threats, and control of corporate assets. Risk acceptance decisions can be transferred to business units that are most affected.

5.1.1 *Systems*

Systems are collections of interrelated parts working together to accomplish one or more objectives. In systems, output is not simply the sum of component parts. There are many systems of interacting parts where viewing the whole tells us more than simply looking at the system's components.[4] Components are affected by being in the system, and the sum of the system output is greater than what the sum of individual outputs would have been without being in the system. Systems are purposeful, meant to do something. The distinction of systems thinking is a focus on the whole, viewing the interactions of structure (system components and relationships), function (outcomes), and process (activities and knowledge).[5] Systems thinking enables understanding the interdependency of those system elements working together in some larger environment. Analysis involves taking systems apart, explaining part behaviors, and aggregating parts back into a whole with better understanding.

Complexities arise in technology.[6] The Internet was created to assure communication links under possible nuclear attack, and have done a very good job at distributing data. It has also led to enormous opportunities to share business data, and led to a vast broadening of the global market. That was an unintended benefit. Some unintended negative aspects include broader distribution of pornography, or expedited communication in illegal or subversive organizations. Three Mile Island in the U.S. saw an interaction of multiple failures in a system that was too tightly coupled.[7] Later, Chernobyl was even worse, as system controls acted counter to solving the problem they were designed to prevent. We try to create self-correcting systems, especially when we want high reliability (nuclear power; oil transportation; airline travel – both in the physical context and in the anti-terrorist context). But it is difficult to make systems foolproof. Especially when systems involve complex, nonlinear interactions, conditions that seem inevitable when people are involved.

5.2 COSO Application of IS Risk Management

COSO involves a risk management framework including the following steps:

1. Internal Environment
2. Objective Setting
3. Event Identification
4. Risk Assessment
5. Risk Response
6. Control Activities
7. Information and Communication
8. Monitoring.

O'Connell provided a systems-based taxonomy for information systems risk management.[8]   The systems view led him to identify factors influencing business process performance in IS grouped into a taxonomy of procedures (design, support, and externalities) and agents (skill, motivation, and information – constituting personnel-related events in the COSO guidelines).

Procedure design requires complete specification of activities needed to correctly   perform the task. It also is necessary to create monitoring capabilities so that management can assure that tasks are being accomplished appropriately. This category in the taxonomy is under procedure support in COSO guidelines.

Procedure support involves the infrastructure of resources and services. This includes appropriate computer technology to communicate with external participants involved, such as vendors or customers. Procedures may require that these external participants be given access through portals, to pass through organizational firewalls. This may seem to lead to a tradeoff between access and security, but industry has generated very effective, secure procedures to allow needed access to systems and information. This category in the taxonomy is under procedure support in COSO guidelines.

Procedure externalities (including external business risks in the COSO guidelines) involve risks from changing economic conditions, competition, disasters (natural and man-made), and changing regulatory controls. Environmental conditions are beyond the control of an organization for the greater part, but risk can be transferred through actions such as insurance, business alliances, and withdrawal from business lines not matching the selected risk appetite of an organization.

Agent skill is the ability to effectively execute procedures. Supervision and training can reduce this class of risk.

Agent motivation is fostered by intrinsic and extrinsic incentives. Risks of insufficient agent motivation for organizational members can be reduced by supervision and incentive programs. Analogous measures for extraorganizational members call for contractual arrangements.

Agent information of sufficient quality and quantity are needed to enable agents to make the best decisions during procedure execution. Procedures involve a series of decisions which can often be automated to gain speed, consistency, and efficiency. Humans are better than computers at making judgments. This judgment can be incorporated into automated systems (in the form of expert systems, for instance), but care must be taken to think of all factors that will be important for future decisions, a daunting task.

Event identification can be accomplished with this taxonomy as a framework as shown in Table 1:

Table 1: Events Threatening Agent Accomplishment of Processes

Component Procedure	Functions	Threat Events
Engage customers / employees	Identify customer groups to target Gather and analyze customer data Anticipate customer preferences Develop marketing initiatives Deliver the message	Target groups not wanting firm's products Target groups unable to afford firm's products Target groups unwilling to travel to firm's locations Customer data not available Inadequate tools for data analysis Inability to identify likely customers Uncertainty of price customers willing to pay Initiatives not deployed at proper time
Provide service employees	Identify services desired Services provided in firm outlets	Lack of knowledge of services to provide Service timing Employee understanding of services / products Services complement marketing
Transact with customers / employees	Pricing Inventory management Delivery checkout services	Prices not competitive Products not optimally priced for profit Store layout not optimized Ineffective store promotions Product mix not optimal Inventory levels not optimal Sales data not effectively captured Information to effectively sell / provide service is not available
Engage customers / employees	Customer response to marketing	Customer does not get the message Message does not provide effective incentives
Provide service to customers	Customer appreciates service initiatives	Customers unaware of available services Customers don't want available services Service delivery unsatisfactory
Transact with customers / employees	Customer value provided	Products hard to locate Product information difficult to locate or understand Products don't meet expectations

(adapted from O'Donnell, 2005)

5.3 IS Risk Identification and Analysis

Information systems involve high levels of risk, in that it is very difficult to predict what problems are going to occur in system development All risks in information system project management cannot be avoided, but early identification of risk can reduce the damage considerably. Kliem and Ludin (1998) gave A risk management cycle[9] consisting of activities managers can undertake to understand what is happening and where:

- Risk Identification
- Risk Analysis
- Risk Control
- Risk Reporting

Risk identification focuses on identifying and ranking project elements, project goals, and risks. Risk identification requires a great deal of pre-project planning and research. Risk analysis is the activity of converting data gathered in the risk identification step into understanding of project risks. Analysis can be supported by quantitative techniques, such as simulation, or qualitative approaches based on judgment. Risk control is the activity of measuring and implementing controls to lessen or avoid the impact of risk elements. This can be reactive, after problems arise, or proactive, expending resources to deal with problems before they occur. Risk reporting communicates identified risks to others for discussion and evaluation.

Risk management in information technology is not a step-by-step procedure, done once and then forgotten. The risk management cycle is a continuous process throughout a project. As the project proceeds, risks are more accurately understood.

The primary means of identifying risk amounts to discussing potential problems with those who are most likely to be involved. Successful risk analysis depends on the personal experience of the analyst, as well as access to the project plan and historical data. Interviews with members of the project team can provide the analyst with the official view of the project, but risks are not always readily apparent from this source. More detailed discussion with those familiar with the overall environment within which the project is implemented is more likely to uncover risks. Three commonly used methods to tap human perceptions of risk are brainstorming, the nominal group technique, and the Delphi method.

5.3.1 *Brainstorming*

Brainstorming involves redefining the problem, generating ideas, and seeking new solutions. The general idea is to create a climate of free association through trading ideas and perceptions of the problem at hand. Better ideas are expected from brainstorming than from individual thought because the minds of more people are tapped. Brainstorming has been proposed for many risk management environments, to tax management.[10] It also applies to information system risk management. The productive thought process works best in an environment where criticism is avoided, or at least dampened.

Group support systems are especially good at supporting the brainstorming process. The feature of anonymity encourages more reticent members of the group to contribute. Most GSSs allow all participants to enter comments during brainstorming sessions. As other participants read these comments, free association leads to new ideas, built upon the comments from the entire group. Group support systems also provide a valuable feature in their ability to record these comments in a file, which can be edited with conventional word-processing software.

An additional feature of most group support systems is the ability for all participants to evaluate the comments and ideas that have been generated by the brainstorming process. By its nature, many of the comments generated will not be useful. The evaluation feature works by allowing each participant to rate each of the other comments on a scale, such as from 1 (for bad) to 10 (for great). Software can average these ratings, and sort comments by these averages. This identifies the most popular ideas.

Brainstorming works best if the group is diverse, and thus more likely to bring different ideas into play. The size of the group should be large enough to allow diversity, but not so large as to cause problems of generating too many comments to handle. The negatives of brainstorming involve the social aspects. Individuals with dominating personalities can take over brainstorming sessions. It is key for productivity to keep the session positive.

5.3.2 *Nominal group technique*

The Nominal Group Technique[11] supports groups of people (ideally seven to ten) who initially write their ideas about the issue in question on a pad of paper. Each individual then presents their ideas, which are recorded on a flip-chart (or comparable computer screen technology). The group can generate new ideas during this phase, which continues until no new ideas are forthcoming. When all ideas are recorded, discussion opens. Each idea is discussed. At the end of discussion, each individual records their evaluation of the most serious risks associated with the project by either rank-ordering or rating.

The silent generation of ideas, and structured discussion are contended to overcome many of the limitations of brainstorming. Nominal groups have been found to yield more unique ideas, more total ideas, and better quality ideas than brainstorming groups.

5.3.3 *Delphi method*

The Delphi method was developed at the RAND Corporation for technological forecasting, but has been applied to many other problem environments. The first phase of the Delphi method is anonymous generation of opinions and ideas related to the issue at hand by participants. These anonymous papers are then circulated to all participants, who revise their thoughts in light of these other ideas. Anonymous ideas are exchanged for either a given number of rounds, or until convergence of ideas.

The Delphi method can be used with any number of participants. Anonymity and isolation allow maximum freedom from any negative aspects of social interaction. On the negative side, the Delphi method is much more time consuming than brainstorming or the nominal group technique. There also is limited opportunity for clarification of ideas. Conflict is usually handled by voting, which may not completely resolve disagreements.

5.3.4 *The systems failure method*

The systems failure method[12] is an approach intended to improve the prospects of success by examining similar undertakings that have failed with the intent of avoiding those things that caused failure. The method consists of studying the process as a system, to enable modeling the system so that cause and effect relationships can be understood. Planned systems are compared with similar systems that have either succeeded or have failed.

The approach begins with gathering as many similar cases as possible. This is a data collection step. Then each case is analyzed with the intent of studying the system aspects similar to the subject. The history of each case is developed, and examined to determine why the system failed. The systems failure approach consists of the following processes:

Systems Failure Method Processes
• **Pre-Analysis**   define purpose, perspectives, gather source material
• **Identify significant failures and select systems**
• **Modeling**   clarify the nature of the system
• **Comparison**   gain understanding
• **Analysis**
• **Synthesis**

Pre-analysis involves conceptualizing the system being studied, to include different viewpoints and perspectives. Information is gathered and analyzed to enable the system components to be identified, their interaction to accomplish system goals, and the hierarchical structure of system control.

Significant failures of similar systems are identified. Failure is the focus of the study. This requires modeling the system in some detail. Many of the more advanced systems involving human interaction consist of ill-structured, messy situations. Soft-systems methodology was proposed[13] as a way to study these systems. Instead of identifying the optimal solution for a system, the purpose of soft systems is to involve users in a learning process. First, understanding of the system is required. The background and history of the problem is useful in gaining understanding. Then, the system is described, and this model of the system can be used to predict the outcome of alternative decisions. Soft systems have been applied in many information system analyses, to include the use of geographic information systems.[14]

Models represent the theory of the analyst about what the results of available actions on the system will be. By studying similar systems, better understanding of the system being studied can be gained. System components need to be described, as well as relationships. Structural relationships describing system behavior are included.

The soft-system methodology consists of seven stages:[15]

---

1. What is the problem situation?
2. Structure the problem situation
3. Identify human activity systems
4. Conceptualize models of human activity systems
5. Compare models with perceptions in the problem situation
6. Identify feasible desirable changes
7. Take action

Stage 1 involves identifying the actors with interests in the situation. Stage 2 requires an analysis of the political aspects of the situation. Systems thinking leads to identification of the system relationships. In stage 4, the analyst develops a model of the system capable of predicting the expected consequences of actions. Stage 5 uses the models to gain insight. Stage 6 involves developing and evaluating more refined alternatives, to include benefit/cost analysis. Finally, the approach leads to action.

Comparison involves identifying what you think would happen with the system being studied, given the model based on similar systems. This requires developing a model laying out the process of system operation, including the decision making subsystem. For instance, a medical information system would need to capture the flow of information and decision making in a medical process. A patient arrives with a malady. Information about this patient's medical history is needed. Records are kept at each medical facility by patient. Those in this medical facility system can be recalled by accessing the database records relating to this patient. The patient is questioned about medical history, and hopefully other sources that might have records are identified and additional records requested. The physician then examines the patient, and diagnoses the causes of the current malady, in light of the historical data available relating to the patient, as well as the physician's knowledge about similar cases. Another database, organized by symptoms, can be accessed by the physician to obtain greater understanding of probable causes. The physician then prescribes a treatment plan, which is closely monitored for results. The overall process requires support in the way of data by patient and data by symptom. That portion of the information system focuses on the patient. Another portion of the information system monitors billing information, to include charges and payment arrangements. The focus of comparison is on decision making and control. Relationships between the system and the wider system are needed, as well as understanding of the effects due to the external environment.

Analysis uses model output to draw inferences about the relationship of actions within the system and expected outcomes. In a medical information system, the administration may use the system to monitor productivity aspects by physicians in attempts to control costs. Physicians can use the system professionally by developing databases by disease and symptom that can be used to determine better treatment plans. **Synthesis** is obtained when the analyst feels that learning about the system has been gained.

Failure of systems is commonly a result of:

- Deficiencies in organizational structure and lack of performance control
- Lack of a clear statement of purpose
- Subsystem deficiencies
- Lack of effective communication between subsystems
- Inadequate design
- Insufficient consideration of environment, and insufficient resources
- Imbalance of resources, and inadequate testing

The systems failure approach can be applied to analyze all types of systems, not just information systems. Lack of a clear statement of purpose appears on their list of causes of failure, further confirming its importance in projects.

System Control: Control is action to reach or maintain a desired state. Classical feedback control monitors the output of the system. When a difference is identified between desired performance levels, such as the size of a ball-bearing being produced, or the characteristics of a microchip, then action is taken by throwing out the inferior product, and adjusting machinery so that future production will be within specifications. A common example of feedback control is a thermostat. More modern forms of feedback control include a model predicting the final form of the output based upon a measurement early in the production process. These systems adjust according to the measures obtained. An example might be a chip in a refrigerator that monitors conditions within the enclosed environment, and contacts the manufacturer's representative to send a repairperson before damage is done. This implies feedforward control, because the outcome of the system is predicted before production actually occurs.

System Communication: Many systems failures are due to problems with communications links between system components. These can be missing links, inadequate links, or links that are not used. There is a vicious circle in organizational communication. Information overload describes situations where so much information is provided that no understanding is obtained. A correction for this condition is to filter communications to those bits that have important information content. However, this of course leads to distortion and omission of some information, some of whichmay turn out to be important. The reaction to this is more messages, which leads inevitably to information overload.

Each of us has to cope with the potential for information overload. Newspapers contain more information each day than any one individual cares to ever know. Therefore, newspapers classify articles by content. Some spend their time reading the front page, others the comics, and yet others concentrate on the sports page. If one can filter out the advertising, the newspaper can be used to gain a good picture of the highlights of what is going on in the world. But modern technology provides even more concentrated news. There are television channels that purvey nothing but news, others that show nothing but cartoons, and others that have sports around the clock. With expanded cable coverage, one can specialize even more. There are headline news channels, and classic sports networks. The age of information overload has certainly arrived.

Human Aspects of Systems: Part of understanding the system is to identify the structure of responsibility – who is responsible for what. Another part of the system is the set of organizational codes of behavior – what is appropriate conduct. Some information is communicable, and some things are not. For instance, in the nuclear energy field, some information is classified by the government. In any organization, some information may well be considered sacrosanct, not to be broadcast. Understanding a system includes understanding what portions of the system are fixed and unchangeable, and what elements are merely there for temporary purposes. For control purposes, understanding the procedure followed to solve problems can be one of the most important system components.

5.4 The Systems View of Enterprise Systems

Enterprise systems (ERP, EIS, other commercially generated acronyms) provide great benefit to organizations, both in business, for profit and non-profit, private sector and public. They integrate previously independent systems, in recognition of the systems aspects of interacting parts providing organizations with data. Data can be generated once, electronically captured for use by all elements of the organization. Enterprise systems also include consideration of the best ways of doing things (processes), which can be reengineered to do things the "right" way (BPR, best practices). Enterprise systems also provide benefit to organizations by reducing the cost of providing information (elimination of duplicate systems, better control of inventory costs, reduced IT staff).

There are negative aspects of enterprise systems as well. They are extremely disruptive. The benefits obtained from BPR and best practices usually require that people in the organization learn new ways to do their jobs. This is for the betterment of the organization, but none of us like to change once we become comfortable in how we do our work. This leads to high levels of turnover in organizations that adopt enterprise systems. In a way, this is self-correcting (system adaption), because those who get with the program and learn the new system become more valuable to the organization, and do more productive work (hopefully leading to greater responsibility and ensuing pay raises), while those who find the new system intolerable take advantage of new employment opportunities elsewhere.

Other disruptive aspects of adopting enterprise systems is that if you adopt vendor best practices, all of your competitors can utilize exactly the same technology that you do. If you are dealing with some chore that does not directly relate to what your organization does extremely well (core competencies), this does not matter. Your organization benefits by lowering the cost and increasing the efficiency of proven methods. On the other hand, if Amazon.com develops a very efficient ordering system internally, they would not want to sacrifice that just to obtain someone else's best practice. If Dell develops a production scheduling system driven by real time orders, they don't want to sacrifice that to adopt what SAP says is the best practice of scheduling. Innovators of core competencies would rather retain their competitive advantage. This leads to a systemic tradeoff. Do you want to modify the vendor enterprise system (customize it), which involves a very high level of complexity in system modification? This leads to a very high cost in software development by the organization, as well as risk of having to redo all of this modification when the vendor drops support of their current software version for a new and improved product version. Or would you rather sacrifice the system you developed and obtain less complexity by living with the vendor system? There is no "right" answer, it depends on the organization's specific situation.

Viewing enterprise software as a system leads to consideration of the risks involved, and the impact on not only IT costs, but also on hidden costs such as organizational disruption, future upgrades, etc. Managerial decision makers can then consider mitigation strategies, important in initial system selection, as well as in developing plans for dealing with contingencies (what to do if the system fails; what to do if the vendor raises the price of software support; what to do if the vendor discontinues support for this version of software). An alternative approach is to avoid all of this hassle, and rent an enterprise system from an application service provider (ASP). That involves a whole new set of systemic risks.

5.4.1 *Alternative ERP forms*

The overall ERP selection decision involves the seven broad categories of alternatives shown in Table 2. Each specific organization might generate variants of selected alternatives that suit their particular needs.

5.4.2 *Outsourcing risks*

Outsourcing has evolved into a way for IT to gain cost savings to organizations. This is true for ERP just as it is for other IT implementations. Competitive pressures as motivation for many organizations to outsource major IT functions.[16] Eliminated jobs make businesses more productive. Often those jobs eliminated are from IT.

Table 2: Alternative ERP Options[17]

Form	Advantages	Disadvantages
In-house	Fit organization	Most difficult, expensive, slowest
In-House + vendor supp.	Blend proven features with organizational fit	Difficult to develop Expensive & slow
Best-of-breed	Theoretically ideal	Hard to link, slow, potentially inefficient
Customize vendor system	Proven features modified to fit organization	Slower, usually more expensive than pure vendor
Select vendor modules	Less risk, fast, inexpensive	If expand, inefficient and higher total cost
Full vendor system	Fast, inexpensive, efficient	Inflexible
ASP	Least risk & cost, fastest	At mercy of ASP

From Olson (2004)

Outsourcing is attractive to many types of organizations, but especially to those that have small IT staffs, without expertise in enterprise systems. Some organizations, such as General Motors, outsource entire IT operations. There also are on-demand application providers willing to provide particular services covering the gamut of IT applications. Reasons for use of an ASP included the need to quickly get a system on-line (even to bridge the period when an internal system is installed), or to cope with IT downsizing. ASPs can help both small carriers develop new capabilities quickly, as well as providing faster implementations at multiple locations for large companies, and provide access to automatic updates and new applications. They also provide a more flexible way to deal with the changing ERP vendor market.

ERP can be outsourced overseas. Overseas outsourcing takes advantage of tremendous cost saving opportunities. As of publication date, India has significant cost advantages over the U.S. and Europe in average programmer salary, while capable of providing equivalent or superior capabilities in many areas. However, relative pay schedules are subject to inflation, and Indian pay rates were expected to increase by double-digit rates over the next few years. ERP skills is one of the areas where higher inflation is expected. However, the expertise available in India still makes them a highly attractive source of IT. Over a period of years, those in other countries such as China are expected to overcome current language barriers and develop sufficiently mature IT skills to draw work from India.

There is a tradeoff in outsourcing ERP systems, in that costs and some form of risks are reduced by outsourcing, but other companies view ERP as too mission-critical to yield control. The biggest risks of outsourcing are downtime and loss of operational data. Organizations whose systems expand rapidly due to acquisition may find outsourcing attractive for technical aspects of ERP. The tradeoff is between savings in capital investment and technical expertise through ASP, versus control and customization abilities better served through in-house IT.

Government use of ERP has its own set of characteristics. The value of outsourcing financial systems in government can be very beneficial in terms of reduced cost.[18] Benefits of application hosting were stated as lower opportunity costs of software ownership, and avoiding problems of developing and retaining IT staff. Additional difficulties faced by governmental IT directors in the governmental sector include the need to be able to defend proposals in public hearings. Such applications also involved the use of ERP to reduce State jobs, which can lead to difficulties with the state information worker union.

5.5 Conclusions

Information systems are crucial to the success of just about every 21st Century organization. The IS/IT industry has moved toward enterprise systems as a means to obtain efficiencies in delivering needed computing support. This approach gains through integration of databases, thus eliminating needless duplication and subsequent confusion from conflicting records. It also involves consideration of better business processes, providing substitution of computer technology for more expensive human labor.

Information technology provides valuable tools enabling organizations of any type to deal with the information revolution more efficiently. Information systems generate vast quantities of data, which often is critical to the organizations they serve. Dealing with data has proven problematic, as organizations that collect data on individuals can not only be used to better serve customers and clients, but also can be targeted by identity thieves and hackers, who create new threats. Furthermore, there is privacy danger in having too much information on individuals centralized for too many purposes. The majority of the public view this data centralization as a prelude to a brave new world of centralized control over all aspects of their lives.

But there are many risks associated with enterprise systems (just as there are with implementing any information technology). Whenever major changes in organizational operation are made, this inherently incurs high levels of risk. COSO frameworks apply to information systems just as they do to any aspect of risk assessment. But specific tools for risk assessment have been developed for information systems. This chapter has sought to consider risks of evaluating IT proposals (focusing on ERP), as well as consideration of IS/IT project risk in general. Methods for identifying risks in IS/IT projects were reviewed, to include brainstorming, nominal group technique, the Delphi method, and the systems failure method.

It helps to design information systems by keeping the idea of general systems in mind. Complex adaptive systems theory offers a great deal of insight into the interrelationships of parts working together for common ends. The COSO framework includes a system of steps for managing risk in information systems. This framework and associated process includes specific threat events for controlling risks of a wide variety.

Endnotes

1. Magnusson, C., Olá, H., Holmqvist, C.S. (2006). The knowledge pressure on risk and security managers is increasing. *Proceedings of the First International Conference on Availability, Reliability and Security (ARES'06)*, IEEE Computer Society, 2-0200 April, 974-979.

2. Edmiston, A.H. (2007). The role of systems and applications monitoring in operational risk management, *BT Technology Journal* 25:1, 68-78.
3. Anderson, K. (2007). Convergence: A holistic approach to risk management, *Network Security* May, 4-7.
4. von Bertalanffy, L. (1968). *General System Theory: Foundations, Development, Applications*, New York: George Brazillier, Inc., revised 1969.
5. Gharajedaghi, J. (1999). *Systems Thinking: Managing Chaos and Complexity*, Woburn, MA: Butturworth-Heinemann.
6. Feenberg, A. (1999). *Questioning Technology*, London: Routledge.
7. Perrow, C. (1999). *Normal Accidents: Living with High-Risk Technologies*, Princeton, NJ: Princeton University Press, reprinted from 1984.
8. O'Donnell, E. (2005). Enterprise risk management: A systems-thinking framework for the event identification phase, *International Journal of Accounting Information Systems* 6, 177-195.
9. From Kliem, R.L., Ludin, I.S. (1998). *Reducing Project Risk*. Aldershot, England: Gower.
10. Beasley, M.S., Jenkins, J.G., Sawyers, R.B. (2006). Brainstorming to identify and manage tax risks. *The Tax Adviser* 37:3, 158-162.
11. Moore, C.M. (1994). *Group Techniques for Idea Building* 2nd ed. Thousand Oaks, CA: Sage Publications.
12. Fortune, J., Peters, G. (1997). *Learning from Failure: The Systems Approach*. New York: John Wiley & Sons.
13. Checkland, P.B. (1981). *Systems Thinking, Systems Practice*. Chichester, England: John Wiley & Sons.
14. Balram, S., Dragićević, S. (2006). Modeling collaborative GIS processes using soft systems theory, UML and object oriented design. *Transactions in GIS* 10:2, 199-218.
15. Khisty, C.J. (1995). Soft-systems methodology as learning and management tool, *Journal of Urban Planning and Development* 121:3, 91-101.
16. Bryson, K.M., Sullivan, W.E. (2003). Designing effective incentive-oriented contracts for application service provider hosting of ERP systems. *Business Process Management Journal* 9(6): 705-721.

17. Derived from Olson, D.L. (2004). *Managerial Issues of Enterprise Resource Planning Systems.* Boston: McGraw-Hill/Irwin.
18. Joplin, B., Terry, C. (2000). Financial system outsourcing: The ERP application hosting option. *Government Finance Review* 16(1) 31-33.

Chapter 6

Disaster Planning

Discusses the implication of risk in human systems
Gives a brief overview of emergency management
Describes information system support to emergency management:
    Databases
    Data mining
    Modeling
    Decision support systems

Life includes many unexpected events, some causing a great deal of damage and inconvenience. Some things we do to ourselves, such as wars. Humans made decisions leading to the London blitz and Hiroshima. Terrorism led to the gassing of the Japanese subway system, to 9/11/2001, to bombings of Spanish and British transportation systems. Some things nature does to us – massive volcanic eruptions, tsunamis, hurricanes and tornados. The SARS virus disrupted public and business activities, particularly in Asia.[1] Some disasters combine human and natural causes – we dam up rivers to control floods, to irrigate, to generate power, and for recreation, as at Johnstown, PA at the turn of the 20th Century. We have developed low-pollution, low-cost electricity through nuclear energy, as at Three-Mile Island in Pennsylvania and Chernobyl. We have built massive chemical plants to produce low cost chemicals, as at Bhopal, India.

Emergency management has been described as the process of coordinating an emergency or its aftermath through communication and organization for deployment and the use of emergency resources.[2] Emergency management is a dynamic process conducted under stressful conditions, requiring flexible and rigorous planning, cooperation, and vigilance. During emergencies, a variety of organizations are often involved. Commercial rivalry can lead to normal competition, rivalry, and mutual distrust. At the governmental level, one would expect cooperation in attaining a common goal, but often so many diverse agencies get involved that attention to the overriding shared goal is dimmed by specific agency goals. Cooperation is also hampered by differences in technology. The focus of this chapter is to review some of the problems involved in disaster planning, as well as review some of the technology tools available to support the disaster planning process.

We have learned to cope and adapt. The old military saying was that the more you sweat in peace, the less you bled in war. Preparation reduces the impact of negative events. Rescue operations at sea and fire stations on land reduce the level of disaster. Police and relief agencies help survivors recover faster. But they need help. The scale of disaster grows as the world's population grows, as humans conquer and damage nature, and as we develop more complex systems.

6.1 Risk Management of Human Systems

Risks exist in every aspect of our lives. In the food production area, science has made great strides in genetic management. But there are concerns about some of the manipulations involved, with different views prevailing across the globe. In the United States, genetic management is generally viewed as a way to obtain better and more productive sources of food more reliably. However, there are strong objections to bioengineered food in Europe and Asia. Some natural diseases, such as mad cow disease, have appeared that are very difficult to control. The degree of control accomplished is sometimes disputed. Europe has strong controls on bioengineering, but even there a pig breeding scandal involving hazardous feed stock and prohibited medications has arisen.[3] Bioengineering risks are important considerations in the food chain.[4] Genetic mapping offers tremendous breakthroughs in the world of science, but involve political risks when applied to human resources management.[5] Even applying information technology to better manage healthcare delivery risks involves risks.[6] Reliance on computer control has been applied to flying aircraft, but hasn't always worked.[7]

6.2 Emergency Management

Local, State and Federal agencies in the United States are responsible for responding to natural and man-made disasters. This is coordinated at the Federal level through the Federal Emergency Management Agency (FEMA). While FEMA has done much good, it is almost inevitable that more is expected of them than they deliver in some cases, such as hurricane recovery in Florida in various years and the Gulf Coast from Hurricane Katrina in 2006. National security is the responsibility of other agencies, military and civilian (Department of Homeland Security – DHS). They are supported by non-governmental agencies such as the American Red Cross. Again, these systems seem to be effective for the greater part, but are not fail-safe, as demonstrated by Pearl Harbor and 9/11/2001.

Disasters are abrupt and calamitous events causing great damage, loss of lives, and destruction. Emergency management is accomplished in every country to some degree. Disasters occur throughout the world, in every form of natural, man-made, and combination of disaster. Disasters by definition are unexpected, and tax the ability of governments and other agencies to cope. A number of intelligence cycles have been promulgated, but all are based on the idea of:

1. Identification of what is not known;
2. Collection – gathering information related to what is not known;
3. Production – answering management questions;
4. Dissemination – getting the answers to the right people.[8]

Information technology has been developing at a very rapid pace, creating a dynamic of its own. Many technical systems have been designed to gather, process, distribute, and analyze information in emergencies. These systems include communications and data. Tools to aid emergency planners communicate include telephones, whiteboards, and the Internet. Tools to aid in dealing with data include database systems (for efficient data organization, storage, and retrieval), data mining tools (to explore large databases), models to deal with specific problems, and combination of these resources into decision support systems to assist humans in reaching decisions quickly or expert systems to make decisions rapidly based on human expertise.

A number of technological systems have been developed to support disaster response. This chapter will focus on the role of information technology in disaster management. We will consider database support, data mining, operations research modeling, and the use of modeling systems to improve disaster response.

6.2.1 *Database support to emergency management*

A starting point to disaster recovery is collection of relevant data. Disaster information management systems (DIMS) have been developed to store such data.[9] A minimum set of requirements for a DIMS are:

1. The ability to recognize and handle different disaster data sources, to include geographical information, registry information, and aid information.
2. The ability to handle disparate disaster data formats. Data can be obtained from diverse data sources to include e-mails, documents, pictures, movies, and audio files.

Some data can be gathered prior to disaster. Geographical data includes information on population, infrastructure, and natural ecosystems. Hazard information is data on the disaster event itself, to include location, severity, and probabilities. Locators are needed to track the current location of victims. Registries are needed to identify victim families, those requiring medical attention, and critical contact information concerning human resources for dealing with various aspects of a disaster. Data can come in many formats. More advanced data types include 3D and virtual reality content. Standardization reduces the difficulties of sharing information.

To prevent accidental or intentional loss of data, and to ensure efficient retrieval and distribution, a centralized data repository (such as a data warehouse) is desirable at a secure location. This will enable more efficient querying of data and thus expedite subsequent analysis. Security calls for a back-up site at a different physical location. Data at both the primary and back-up sites should be periodically monitored for accuracy and operational readiness. Some of the data stored in these systems may be sensitive, to include critical national infrastructure content concerning transportation, power, and communication networks, as well as military facilities. Individual information can also be sensitive, such as personal identification data that might lead to compromise by identity thieves (social security numbers, etc.), or sensitive medical information on individuals. Access management and encryption systems exist to safeguard such data, but these systems need to be properly implemented.

Some geographical data needs to be constantly updated for location. Critical assets may be moving quite often in a disaster situation. Part of the dynamic of life is the constant development of new technologies.

6.2.2 *Data mining*

Data mining is the analysis of large scale databases by computer software applying statistical and/or artificial intelligence tools with the intent of exploring data to identify patterns or other useful relationships. Data mining is a technological response to the masses of data generated by rapidly expanding data storage and manipulation capabilities. Data mining has been utilized in all aspects of governmental and other emergency management venues. Hale (2006) sought to develop and test the feasibility of a comprehensive open source intelligence relational database for the study of terrorism, intended for data mining.[10] Past intelligence efforts in the U.S. involved fragmented approaches as different agencies were responsible for domestic and foreign threats, law enforcement versus national security, and peacetime operations versus wartime. There had been a general lack of data sharing among data collection agencies and intelligence users.[11]

Open source intelligence would better support delivery of critical information to emergency management. It was intended to access all types of media, to include government reports, scientific research, commercial information vendor input, and the Internet. Data included was to include sources that were not clandestine, nor from illegal sources. Data also is declassified, allowing efficient transfer to emergency management operatives at all levels and across international borders.

Terrorists have been able to utilize the power of the Internet in many ways.[12] The Internet provides easy access with limited regulations, huge audiences, anonymous communication for the most part, and a multimedia environment. Terrorist groups can place information to include history and organizational activities, current news, opinion pieces, training manuals, and fundraising material. Chat rooms have been used by Hamas to plan operations. The Internet has been cited as al-Qaeda's most effective means of communicating and coordinating their activities.[13]

Hale cites arguments that intelligence failures can be overcome through information and communication technologies,[14] which include computers, satellites, and undersea communication technology. Many resources have been directed to intelligence. One popular idea is that centralizing data collection will lead to greater efficiency. The Terrorist Screening Center was created to collect, consolidate, and maintain terrorist suspect watch lists from nine federal agencies, to include the FBI, Department of Homeland Security, Department of Defense, and Department of State. Whether centralization will automatically lead to greater efficiency is an open question. One study revealed that many agencies lacked sharing policies, and others who were willing to share could not due to incompatible software and database systems that were excessively labor intensive.[15]

Other problems exist from a wealth of data. The USA Patriot Act expanded the use of wiretapping and other intelligence collection methods. This has led to information overload as governmental agencies seek to absorb new information.[16] Coping with open source data has also been a challenge. After September 11, 2001, a tremendous volume of terrorism-related data flooded the system, which was of course unprepared for organizing and classifying it into a meaningful body of information.[17] In order to analyze and disseminate useful content, methodologies were needed to identify, model, and predict relationships among terrorists. Many data sources at that time were posted on the Internet. However, none provided codebooks, over one-half offered no consistent definitions of their terms, several lacked basic search capabilities, and all focused on international terrorism.[18]

Even in environments with well-established data collection and information sharing systems face challenges, primarily from lack of interoperability of systems.[19] Traffic incident management is a well-known problem, applying to every community. Computer Aided Dispatch (CAD) systems have been in place since the 1970s to track status of field units and incidents. These systems retrieve and store critical information in support of police, fire, and emergency medical support. They have led to reduced response time, increased dispatcher efficiency, and a centralized location for timely, accurate, and secure information. However, almost every CAD has unique features, and it is very difficult to link systems. Barriers to integration include local agency resistance to change, security concerns, and differences in system development eras.

6.2.3 *Modeling*

There are many modeling tools that can be used for specific problems. Operations research has developed a wide variety of analytic tools, capable of dealing with situations involving certainty or probability. If data is certain, it is often possible to develop optimization models, to identify the best combination of products to manufacture, as in automobile assembly lines, oil refineries, or breakfast cereal plants. If data is probabilistic, it is much harder to find the best possible solution to a given problem, but it is usually possible to predict the performance of a given system. There are tools that can deal with uncertain situations, but they have to be based on subjective inputs.

Monte Carlo simulation is a very useful tool to predict performance of systems involving probabilistic data. It has been widely applied to emergency management, to include better understanding hazards, comparing alternative strategies, improving system operation and coordination, and developing and assessing evacuation plans.[20] For instance, Alachua County, Florida's Emergency Management

Department used an integer programming model to locate their disaster recovery centers. The project was cited as an outstanding project providing the Office of Emergency Management with tangible results based on careful research and problem solving rather than guesses.[21]

6.2.4 *Emergency management support systems*

A number of software products have been marketed to support emergency management. These are often various forms of a decision support system. The Department of Homeland Security in the U.S. developed a National Incident Management System. A similar system used in Europe is the Global Emergency Management Information Network Initiative.[22] While many systems are available, there are many challenges due to unreliable inputs at one end of the spectrum, and overwhelmingly massive data content at the other extreme.

Decision support systems (DSS) have been in existence since the early 1970s.[23] A general consensus is that DSSs consist of access to tailored data and customized models with real-time access for decision makers. With time, as computer technology has advanced and as the Internet has become available, there is a great deal of change in what can be accomplished. Database systems have seen tremendous advances since the original concept of DSS. Now weather data from satellites can be stored in data warehouses, as can masses of point-of-sale scanned information for retail organizations, and output from enterprise information systems for internal operations. Many kinds of analytic models can be applied, ranging from spreadsheet models through simulations and optimization models. While the idea of DSS is now over 30 years old, it can still be very useful in support of emergency management. It still can take the form of customized systems accessing specified data from internal and external sources as well as a variety of models suitable for specific applications needed in emergency management situations. The focus is still on supporting humans making decisions. If problems can be so structured that computers can operate on their own (Hal in 2001 comes to mind), decision support systems evolve into expert systems. Expert systems can and have also been used to support emergency management.

Systems in place for emergency management include the U.S. National Disaster Medical System (NDMS), providing virtual centers designed as a focal point for information processing, response planning, and inter-agency coordination. Systems have been developed for forecasting earthquake impact[24] or the time and size of bioterrorism attacks.[25] This demonstrates the need for DSS support not only during emergencies, but also in the planning stage.

6.3 Conclusions

Emergencies can arise in two types. One is repetitive – hurricanes have hammered the Gulf Coast of the U.S. throughout history, and will continue to do so (just as tornadoes will hit the Midwest and typhoons the Pacific). A great deal of experience and data can be gathered for those events. Our weather forecasting systems have done a very good job of providing warning systems for actual events over the short term of hours and days. However, humans will still be caught off-guard, as with Hurricane Katrina. The other basic type of emergencies are surprises. These can be natural (such as the tsunami of 2005) or human-induced, such as September 11, 2001. We cannot hope to anticipate, nor will we find it economic to massively prepare for every surprise. We don't think that a good asteroid-collision-prevention system would be a wise investment of our national resources. On the other hand, there is growing support for an effective global warming prevention system.

The first type of emergency is an example of risk – we have data to estimate probabilities. The second type is an example of uncertainty – we can't accurately estimate probabilities for the most part. (People do provide estimates of the probability of asteroid collision, but the odds are so small that they don't register in our minds. Global warming probabilities are near certainty, but the probability of a compensating cooling event in the near future evades calculation.)

Thus the crux of the problem in supporting emergency management is that tools exist to gather data, and tools such as data mining exist to try to make some sense of it, but the problem is that we usually won't have the particular data that will be useful to make decisions in real time. It is also reasonably certain that after any event, critics will be able to review what data was available and point to tell-tale information that could have enlightened decision makers at the time but didn't. After World War II, the U.S. was flooded with people who thought that the U.S. Navy should have known the Japanese would bomb Pearl Harbor. CNN and national networks have very predictable scripts for every emergency, with reporters playing to the camera, pointing out the gross malfeasance of those in control in not knowing, preparing for, and countering whatever happened. That's how they raise their ratings – the audience likes conspiracy theories. But having data is not enough – human minds have to comprehend the core information, and the more information that is provided, the harder that is. The solution is not LESS information, but some filters to focus on the critical core would be. The next problem is that how to make such filters is unknown, especially in new problem domains.

Emergency management is thus a no-win game. However, someone has to do it. They need to do the best they can in preplanning:

1. gathering and organizing data likely to be pertinent;
2. developing action plans that can be implemented at the national, regional, and local level;
3. organizing people into teams to respond nationally, regionally, and locally, trained to identify events, and to respond with all needed systems (rescue, medical, food, transportation, control, etc.).

Information technology can be of best use in gathering and organizing data. But systems also need to be easy to use during crises. The tradeoff is that the more comprehensive the data that is contained, the more difficult they are to use.

Endnotes

1. Tan, W.-J., Enderwick, P. (2006). Managing threats in the global era: The impact and response to SARS, *Thunderbird International Business Review* 48:4, 515-536.

2. Alexander, D. (2003). Towards the development of standards in emergency management training and education, *Disaster Prevention and Management* 12, 113-123.
3. Suder, G., Gillingham, D.W. (2007). Paradigms and paradoxes of agricultural risk governance, *International Journal of Risk Assessment and Management* 7:3, 444-457.
4. Reilly, L.A., Courtenay, O. (2007). Husbandry practices, badger sett density and habitat composition as risk factors for transient and persistent bovine tuberculosis on UK cattle farms, *Preventive Veterinary Medicine* 80:2-3, 129-142; Fletcher, A.L. (2007). Reinventing the pig: The negotiation of risks and rights in the USA xenotransplantation debate, *International Journal of Risk Assessment and Management* 7:3, 341-349.
5. Markel, K.S., Barclay, L.A. (2007). The intersection of risk management and human resources: An illustration using genetic mapping, *International Journal of Risk Assessment and Management* 7:3, 326-340.
6. Smaltz, D.H., Carpenter, R., Saltz, J. (2007). Effective IT governance in healthcare organizations: A tale of two organizations, *International Journal of Healthcare Technology and Management* 8:1/2, 20-41.
7. Dalcher, D. (2007). Why the pilot cannot be blamed: A cautionary note about excessive reliance on technology, *International Journal of Risk Assessment and Management* 7:3, 350-366.
8. Mueller, R.S. III (2004). The FBI, *Vital Speeches of the Day* 71:4, 106-109.
9. Ryoo, J., Choi, Y.B. (2006). A comparison and classification framework for disaster information management systems, *International Journal of Emergency Management* 3:4, 264-279.
10. Hale, W.C. (2006). Information versus intelligence: Construction and analysis of an open source relational database of worldwide extremist activity, *International Journal of Emergency Management* 3:4, 280-297.
11. Cilluffo, F.J., Marks, R.A., Salmoiraghi, G.C. (2002). The use and limits of US intelligence, *The Washington Quarterly* 25, 61-74.

12. Weimann, G. (2004). *How Modern Terrorism Uses the Internet.* Washington, DC: United States Institute of Peace, Special Report No. 116.
13. Katz, R. (2005). Tools of the trade: Hunting terrorists, *Crime and Justice International* 20, 19.
14. Hale (2006), op cit.
15. United States General Accounting Office (2003). Homeland security: Efforts to improve information sharing need to be strengthened, *Report to the Secretary of Homeland Security.* Washington: GAO-03-760.
16. Dearstyne, B.W. (2002). Information and the war on terrorism: Issues and opportunities, *Information Outlook* 6:3, 14-18.
17. Reid, E., Qin, W., Chung, W., Xu, J., Zhou, Y., Schumaker, R., Sageman, M., Chen, H. (2004). Terrorism knowledge discovery project: A knowledge discovery approach to addressing the threats of terrorism, *Proceedings of the Second Symposium on Intelligence and Security Informatics.* Tucson: University of Arizona, 125-145.
18. Buchalter, A.R., Curtis, G.E. (2003). *Inventory and Assessment of Databases Relevant for Social Science Research on Terrorism.* Washington: Federal Research Division, Library of Congress.
19. Salasznyk, P.P., Lee, E.E., List, G.F., Wallace, W.A. (2006). A systems view of data integration for emergency response, *International Journal of Emergency Management* 3:4, 313-331.
20. Ni, D. (2006). Challenges and strategies of transportation modeling and simulation under extreme conditions, *International Journal of Emergency Management* 3:4, 298-312.
21. Dekle, J., Lavieri, M.S., Martin, E., Emir-Farinas, H., Francis, R.L. (2005). A Florida county locates disaster recovery centers, *Interfaces* 35:2, 133-139.
22. Thompson, S., Altay, N., Green, W.G. III, Lapetina, J. (2006). Improving disaster response efforts with decision support systems, *International Journal of Emergency Management* 3:4, 250-263.
23. Gorry and Scott Morton

24. Aleskerov, F., Say, A.L., Toker, A., Akin, H.L., Altay, G. (2005). A cluster-based decision support system for estimating earthquake damage and casualties, *Disasters* 3, 255-276.
25. Walden, J., Kaplan, E.H. (2004). Estimating time and size of a bioterror attack, *Emergency Infectious Disease* 1:7.

PART II: Tools

Chapter 7

Balanced Scorecard

Describes the concept of balanced scorecards
Describes balanced scorecards in the context of enterprise risk
   management
Demonstrates the method by applying balanced scorecards to credit
   data

It is essential use models to handle risk in enterprises. Risk-tackling models can be

1) an analytical method for valuing instruments, measuring risk and/or attributing regulatory or economic capital;
2) an advanced or complex statistical or econometric method for parameter estimation or calibration used in the above; or
3) a statistical or analytical method for credit risk rating or scoring.

Many risk studies in banking involving analytic (quantitative) models have been presented.[1] Value-at-Risk models have been popular,[2] partially in response to Basel II banking guidelines. Other analytic approaches include simulation of internal risk rating systems using past data. Swedish banks were found to use credit rating categories, and that each bank reflected it's own risk policy.[3] One bank was found to have a higher level of defaults, but without adversely affecting profitability due to constraining high risk loans to low amounts. Systemic risk from overall economic systems as well as risk from networks of banks with linked loan portfolios has been modeled.[4] Overall economic system risk was found to be much more likely, while linked loan portfolios involved high impact but very low probability of default.

The use of scorecards has been popularized by Kaplan and Norton in their balanced scorecard,[5] as well as other similar efforts to measure performance on multiple attributes.[6] In the Kaplan and Norton framework, four perspectives are used, each with possible goals and measures specific to each organization. Table 1 demonstrates this concept:

Table 1: Balanced Scorecard Perspectives, Goals, and Measures

Perspectives	Goals	Measures
FINANCIAL	Survive Succeed Prosper	Cash flow Quarterly sales, growth, operating income by division Increase in market share, Increase in Return on Equity
CUSTOMER	New products Responsive supply Preferred suppliers Customer partnerships	% sales from new products, %sales from proprietary products On-time delivery (customer definition) Share of key accounts' purchases, ranking by key accounts # of cooperative engineering efforts
INTERNAL BUSINESS	Technology capability Manufacturing excellence Design productivity New product innovation	Benchmark vs. competition Cycle time, unit cost, yield Silicon efficiency, engineering efficiency Schedule: actual vs. planned
INNOVATION & LEARNING	Technology leadership Manufacturing learning Product focus Time to market	Time to develop next generation Process time to maturity % products equaling 80% of sales New product introduction vs. competition

This framework of measures was proposed as a means to link intangible assets to value creation for shareholders. Scorecards provide a focus on strategic objectives (goals) and measures, and have been applied in many businesses and governmental organizations with reported success. The use of balanced scorecards in the context of risk management has been proposed.[7] Specific applications to,[8] homeland security,[9] and auditing[10] have been proposed.

Model risk pertains to the risk that models are either incorrectly implemented (with errors) or that make use of questionable assumptions, or assumptions that no longer hold in a particular context. It is the responsibility of the executive management in charge of areas that develop and/or use models to determine to what models this policy applies.

Lhabitant summarized a series of cases where model risk led to large banking losses.[11] These models vary from trading model in pricing stripped mortgage-backed securities to Risk and Capital Models in deciding on the structured securities to decision models in issuing a gold card. Table 2 summarizes some model risk events in banking.

Table 2: Model Risk Events in Banking

Model	Trading and position management models	Decision models in retail banking	Risk and Capital Models
Model Risk	booking with a model that does not incorporate all features of the deal; booking with an unvetted or incorrect model; incorrect estimation of model inputs (parameters); incorrect calibration of the model; etc.	incorrect statistical projections of loss making an incorrect decision (e.g. lending decision) incorrectly calculating and reporting the Bank's risk (e.g. default and loss estimation) as a result of an inadequate model, etc.	use of an unvetted or incorrect model; poor or incorrect estimation of model parameters; testing limitations due to a lack of historic data; weak or missing change control processes, etc.

Sources of model risk arise from the incorrect implementation and/or use of a performing model (one with good predictive power) or the correct implementation/use of a non-performing model (one with poor predictive power). To address these risks vetting of a statistical model is comprised of two main components: Vetting and Validation.[12] Vetting focuses on analytic model components, includes a methodology review, and verifies any implementation, while Validation follows vetting and is an ongoing systematic process to evaluate model performance and to demonstrate that the final outputs of the model are suitable for the intended business purpose.

7.1 Demonstration of ERM Balanced Scorecard

ERM and balanced scorecard systems have been noted to share many elements.[13] These include:

- **Focus on strategy**
- **Holistic perspective**
- **Emphasis on interrelationships**
- **Top-down emphasis**
- **Desire for consistency**
- **Focus on accountability**
- **Continuous process.**

A framework of balanced scorecard for ERM can include different perspectives. For instance,

- **Customer perspective** – goals and measures focusing on how the organization should appear to its customers;
- **Financial perspective** – goals and measures focusing on how the organization should appear to its stakeholders;
- **Learning and Growth perspective** – goals and measures of how the ability to change and improve can be sustained;
- **Internal Business perspective** – goals and measures for excelling in business processes to satisfy stakeholders and customers.

Example goals and measures are given in Table 3:

Table 3: Conventional Balanced Scorecard[14]

Perspective	Vision Achievement	Goals	Measures
Customer satisfaction	Appear to customers	Improve product / service quality Improve delivery timeliness Improve perception of value	Number of customer contact points Delivery time Customer scores
Financial performance	Appear to shareholders	Higher profit Improved cash flow Revenue growth	Profit by supply chain partner Net cash generated throughout supply chain Increase in customers and sales Percentage return on assets
Learning & Growth	Ability to change & improve	Increase employee ownership Improve information flow Increase employee identification of disruptions	Employee survey scores Changes in reports, report frequency Compare actual disruptions with reports of potential
Internal Business Processes	Excel to satisfy stakeholders & customers	Reduce waste Shorten start-to-finish time Cost reduction	Scrap by weight or product Time from raw material to delivery to customer Unit costs

Enterprise Risk Management

Table 4: ERM Balanced Scorecard[15]

Perspective	Vision Achievement	Goals	Measures
Customer satisfaction	Appear to customers	Reduce customer defections Monitor threats to reputation Increase customer feedback about threats	Number of customers retained Negative press coverage Customer surveys comparing delivery to that of competitors
Financial performance	Appear to shareholders	Reduce threats from price competition Reduce cost overruns Reduce external cost due to supply chain processes	Customer defections due to price Surcharges, holding costs, overtime Warranty claims, legal costs, sales returns
Learning & Growth	Ability to change & improve	Increase employee awareness of risks Increase supplier accountability for disruptions Increase employee awareness of supply chain risks relative to other risks	Number of employees attending risk management training Contract provisions addressing accountabilities & penalties Number of departments attending risk identification and assessment workshops
Internal Business Processes	Excel to satisfy stakeholders & customers	Reduce probability & impact of threats Identify specific tolerances for risk Reduce risk exchanges to other processes	Number of employees attending risk management training Number of process variances exceeding acceptable Extent of risks realized in other functions

The conventional use of balanced scorecard focuses on goal statements and measures as tangible as possible of their attainment. This has proven to be a useful means to coordinate attention within organizations on those aspects of operations that management has identified as critical to organizational performance. The same can be done for enterprise risk management. Table 4 gives one possible set of goals and measures.

This approach can be effective in focusing organization attention on enterprise risk management.

7.2 Case Study: Credit Scorecard Validation

The section aims to validate the predictive Scorecard that is currently being used in a big bank. By breaking-up funded accounts into 3 samples based on their limit issue date, the model's ability to rank order accounts based on creditworthiness was validated for individual sample and compared to the Credit Bureau Score. Tables 5, 6 and 7 give the sample size, mean and standard deviation of these three samples. Sample 1 involves accounts from January 1999 to June 1999, Sample 2 involves accounts from July 1999 to December 1999 and Sample 3 involves accounts from January 2000 to June 2000. Cases 90 days delinquent or worse, accounts closed with a "NA (non-accrual)" status or that were written-off were included as bad performance. Good cases were defined as those that did not meet the bad definition. The bad definition is evaluated at 18 months. Three samples of cohorts have been created and compared. Specified time periods refer to month-end dates. For the performance analyses, the limit issue dates will be considered, while the population and characteristic analyses will use the application dates. In order to validate the relative effectiveness of the Scorecard, we conduct statistic analysis and report results for the following statistical measures: Divergence Test, Kolmogorov-Smirnov (K-S) Test, Lorenz Curve, and population stability index.

7.2.1 *Statistical results and discussion*

Table 5 presents the summary analysis for performance samples. The Lorenz Curves are depicted in Figures 1, 2, 3 and 4 show scorecard

Table 5: Summary for Performance Samples

		Jan-Jun 99	Jul-Dec 99	Jan-Jun 00
Good	N	26,783	20,849	23,941
	Mean	250	248	246
	Std. Dev	24	24	24
Bad	N	317	307	533
	Mean	228	231	225
	Std. Dev	23	23	21
Total	N	27,100	21,156	24,474
	Mean	249	248	245
	Std. Dev	24	24	24
KS	KS Value	39	33	38
	Score	240	246	239
Divergence		0.869	0.528	0.843
Bad%		1.17	1.45	2.18
* Low Score Override		574	504	533
** Instore accounts		459	569	1,353

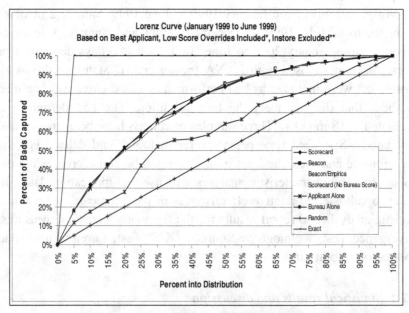

Note: Based on Best Applicant, Low Score Overrides Included, Instore Excluded

Figure 1: January 1999 – June 1999 Performance Sample: Lorenz Curve

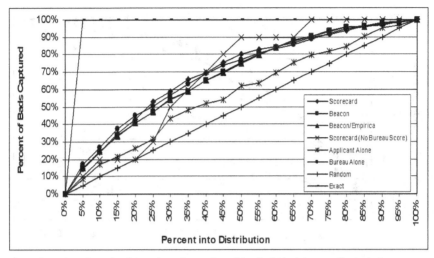

Note: Based on Best Applicant, Low Score Overrides Included, Instore Excluded

Figure 2: July 1999 – December 1999 Performance Sample: Lorenz Curve

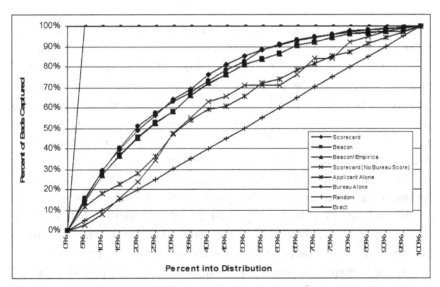

Note: Based on Best Applicant, Low Score Overrides Included, Instore Excluded

Figure 3: January 2000 – June 2000 Performance Sample: Lorenz Curve

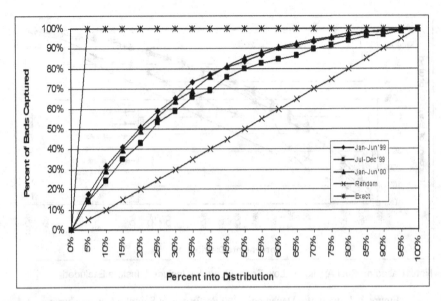

Figure 4: Comparison of Performance Samples: Jan 99-Jun 99 vs. Jul 99 Dec 99 vs. Jan 00-Jun 00

performance validation for Jan 1999-June 1999, July 1999-December 1999 and January 2000- June 2000 respectively. In a data set that has been sorted by the scores in ascending order (if a low score corresponds to a risky account), the perfect model would capture all the 'bads' as quickly as possible. The Lorenz Curve assesses a model's ability to effectively rank order these accounts. For example, if 15% of the accounts were bad, the ideal or exact model would capture all these bads within the 15th percentile of the Score Distribution (the x-axis).

The results demonstrate the Scorecard is a good predictor of risk. Amongst the 3 selected sampling periods, the two cohorts of Jan-99 to Jun-99 and Jan-00 to Jun-00 highlight a slightly better predictive ability than the cohort of Jul-99 to Dec-99. Scorecard also performs better than, though not by a significant margin, the Credit Bureau Score.

The performance statistics for the three selected samples as provided in Table 5, 6 and 7 indicate the superiority of the Scorecard as a predictive tool.

The Scorecard was found to be a more effective assessor of risk for the earlier sample, Jan-99 to Jun-99, then the latest sample, Jan-00 to Jul-00, but was slightly less effective for the Jul-99 to Dec-99 sample. There was a more distinct separation between 'goods' and 'bads' for the above-mentioned first 2 samples than the last: the maximum difference between the 'good' and 'bad' cumulative distributions was 39% and 38% respectively, versus 33% for the remaining sample. Similarly, the divergence values were 0.869 and 0.843, versus 0.528 for the less effective sample.

It is possible that the Scorecard was better able to separate 'good' accounts from 'bad' ones for the earlier sample. On the other hand, the process to clean-up delinquent Unsecured Line of Credit accounts starting from mid-2001 may result to more bad observations for the latest sample (those accounts booked between Jan-00 to Jun-00 with a 18-months observation window will catch up with this clean up process). This can be evidenced by the bad rate of 2.18% for the Jan-00 to Jun-00 sample, compared to 1.45% for the Jul-99 to Dec-99 sample, and 1.17% for the Jan-99 to Jun-99 sample. If most of these bad accounts in the clean-up have a low initial score, the predictive ability of the Scorecard on this cohort will be increased.

7.2.2 *Population distributions and stability*

We conduct a comparison between the initial sample used to develop the model and subsequent sampling periods, which provides insight into whether or not the scorecard is being used to score a different population. The analyses considered All applicants are included, but outliers have been excluded, i.e., invalid scorecard points. We consider four sampling periods for the Cumulative and Interval Population Distribution Charts: the FICO development sample, Jan-99 to Jun-99, Jul-99 to Dec-99, and Jan-00 to Jul-00 (see Figures 5 and 6). We can see a very notable population shift across the samples where the recent applicants clearly were scoring lower point than before. On the other hand, the Development sample was markedly distinct from the three selected samples.

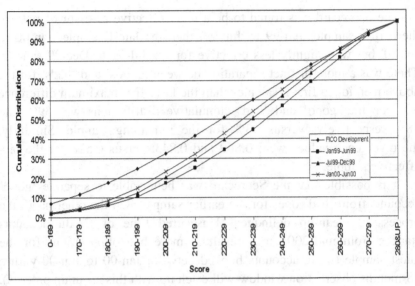

Note: Based on Best Applicant, Instore Excluded

Figure 5: Cumulative Population Distribution on all Applicants

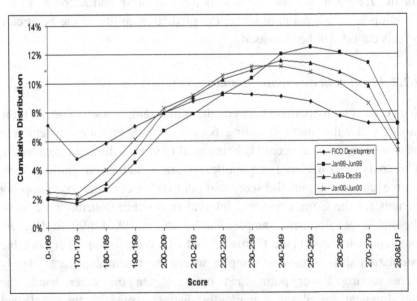

Note: Based on Best Applicant, Instore Excluded

Figure 6: Interval Population Distribution on All Applications

We now use the population stability index to estimate the change between the samples. As mentioned above, a stability index of < 0.10 indicates an insignificant shift, 0.10 - 0.25 requires some investigation and > 0.25 means that a major change has taken place between the populations being compared. Computation found that the indexes for the 3 samples on funded accounts are greater than 0.1, and the more recent samples scores a lower index than the older samples: 0.2027 for the Jan-99 to Jun-99 sample, 0.1461 for the Jul-99 to Dec-99 sample, and 0.1036 for the Jan-00 to Jun-00 sample. We also compute the monthly Population Stability which shows the monthly index for total applications (funded or not funded) in the past two years starting from Jan-00. This result further confirms on the declining trend with the monthly indexes for the past 20 months all rest within 0.1.

The stability indices revealed that the greatest population shift occurred when the Scorecard was originally put in place, then the extent of shift reduced gradually across time. The indexes stayed within 0.1 for the past 20 months.

7.3 Conclusion

Maintaining a certain level of risk has become a key strategy to make profits in today's economy.

Risk in enterprise can be quantified and managed using various models. Models also provide support to organizations seeking to control enterprise risk. We have discussed risk modeling and reviewed some common risk measures. Using the variation of these measures, we demonstrate support to risk management through validation of predictive scorecards for a large bank. The scorecard model is validated and compared to credit bureau scores.

A comparison of the KS value and the divergence value between Scorecard and Bureau Score in the three samples indicated Scorecard is a better tool than Bureau Score to distinguish the 'bads' from the 'goods'. On the other hand, there was a difference between the Indirect Scorecard and the Direct Scorecard, as the Direct Scorecard identified bad accounts at a slightly quicker rate than Bureau Score. This was because the

Scorecard incorporated numerous Bureau attributes. Vetting and validation of models may encounter many challenges in practice. For example, when retail models under vetting are relatively new to the enterprise, when there are large amounts of variables and data to manipulate and limited access to these datasets due to privacy restrictions, when validation tests are not standardized and there are demands to change measures if results do not look favorable, these challenges become apparent.

Endnotes

1. Crouhy, M., Galai, D., Mark, R. (2000). A comparative analysis of current credit risk models, *Journal of Banking & Finance* 24, 59-117; Crouhy, M., Galai, D., Mark, R. (1998). Model Risk, *Journal of Financial Engineering* 7:3/4, 267-288, reprinted in Model Risk: Concepts, Calibration and Pricing, (ed. R. Gibson), *Risk Book*, 2000, 17- 31.

2. Alexander, G.J., Baptista, A.M. (2004). A comparison of VaR and CVaR constraints on portfolio selection with the mean-variance model. *Management Science* 50:9, 1261-1273; Chavez-Demoulin, V., Embrechts, P., Nešlehová, J. (2006). Quantitative models for operational risk: Extremes, dependence and aggregation. *Journal of Banking & Finance* 30, 2635-2658; Garcia, R., Renault, É, Tsafack, G. (2007). Proper conditioning for coherent VaR in portfolio management. *Management Science* 53:3, 483-494; Taylor, N. (2007). A note on the importance of overnight information in risk management models. *Journal of Banking & Finance* 31, 161-180.

3. Jacobson, T., Lindé, J., Roszbach, K. (2006). Internal ratings systems, implied credit risk and the consistency of banks' risk classification policies. *Journal of Banking & Finance* 30, 1899-1926.

4. Elsinger, H., Lehar, A., Summer, M. (2006). Risk assessment for banking systems. *Management Science* 52:9, 1301-1314.

5. Kaplan, R.S., Norton, D.P. (1992). The balanced scorecard – Measures that drive performance. *Harvard Business Review* 70:1, 71-79; Kaplan, R.S., Norton, D.P. (2006). *Alignment: Using the*

Balanced Scorecard to Create Corporate Synergies. Cambridge, MA: Harvard Business School Press Books.

6. Bigio, D., Edgeman, R.L., Ferleman, T. (2004). Six sigma availability management of information technology in the Office of the Chief Technology Officer of Washington, DC. *Total Quality Management* 15(5-6), 679-687; Scandizzo, S. (2005). Risk mapping and key risk indicators in operational risk management. *Economic Notes by Banca Monte dei Paschi di Siena SpA* 34:2, 231-256.

7. Papalexandris, A., Ioannou, G., Prastacos, G., Soderquist, K.E. (2005). An integrated methodology for putting the balanced scorecard into action. *European Management Journal* 23:2, 214-227; Calandro, J., Jr., Lane, S. (2006). An introduction to the enterprise risk scorecard. *Measuring Business Excellence* 10:3, 31-40.

8. Anders, U., Sandstedt, M. (2003). An operational risk scorecard approach. *Risk* 16:1, 47-50; Wagner, H. (2004). The use of credit scoring in the mortgage industry. *Journal of Financial Services Marketing* 9:2, 179-183.

9. Caudle, S. (2005). Homeland security. *Public Performance & Management Review* 28:3, 352-375.

10. Herath, H.S.B., Bremser, W.G. (2005). Real-option valuation of research and development investments: Implications for performance measurement. *Managerial Auditing Journal* 20:1, 55-72.

11. Lhabitant, F. (2000). Coping with model risk, in *The Professional Handbook of Financial Risk Management*, M. Lore, L. Borodovsky (eds), Butterworth-Heinemann.

12. Sobehart, J., Keenan, S. (2001). Measuring Default Accurately, *Credit Risk Special Report, Risk* 14, 31–33.

13. Beasley, M., Chen, A., Nunez, K., Wright, L. (2006). Working hand in hand: Balanced scorecards and enterprise risk management. *Strategic Finance* 87:9, 49-55.

14. Developed from content provided in Beasley et al. (2006).

15. Developed from content provided in Beasley et al. (2006).

Chapter 8

Multiple Criteria Analysis

> Describes options for obtaining enterprise information systems
>   Addresses risks involved with these options
>   Identifies tradeoffs among these benefits and risks
> Describes multiple criteria decision making models
> Demonstrates the SMART method for selection decisions involving
>   risk

This chapter discusses analysis of decisions involving multiple criteria. It is applied in the context of ERP. An organization is facing the decision of the form of ERP system to adopt.

A particular ASP might be attractive as a source for ERP. These include the opportunity to open new lines of business, and opportunities to gain market-share with minimal short-term risk. Some organizations may also view ASPs as a way to aid cash flow in periods when they are financially weak and desperate for business.[1]

There are risks in outsourcing. In many cases, cost rise precipitously after the outsourcing firm has become committed to the relationship. One explanation given was the lack of analytical models and tools to evaluate alternatives. These tradeoffs are recapitulated in Table 1:

Table 1: Factors for and Against Outsourcing ERP[2]

Reasons to Outsource	Reasons Against Outsourcing
Reduced capital expenditure for ERP software and updates	Security and privacy concerns
Lower costs gained through ASP economies of scale (efficiency)	Concern about vendor dependency and lock-in
More flexible and agile IT capability	Availability, performance and reliability concerns
Increased service levels at reasonable cost	High migration costs
Expertise availability unaffordable in-house (eliminate the need to recruit IT personnel)	ERP expertise is a competency critical to organizational success
Allowing the organization to focus on their core business	ERP systems are inextricably tied to IT infrastructure
Continuous access to the latest technology	Some key applications may be in-house and critical
Reduced risk of infrastructure failure	Operations are currently as efficient as the ASPs
Manage IT workload variability	Corporate culture doesn't deal well with working with partners
Replace obsolete systems	

Bryson and Sullivan noted reasons that an ASP might shirk their commitments, such as ASP success, or conversely ASP bankruptcy. Their site might be attacked and vandalized, or destroyed by natural disaster. Each organization must balance these factors and make their own decision. The following cases demonstrate two organizations that reached different conclusions.

8.1 Selection Decision Methods

The ideal theoretical approach is a rigorous cost/benefit study, in net present terms. Methods supporting this positivist view include cost/benefit analysis, applying net present value, calculating internal rate of return or payback. These methods are widely known.[3] Many academics as well as consulting practitioners take the position that this is crucial. However, nobody really has a strong grasp on predicting the future in a dynamic environment such as ERP, and practically, complete analysis in economic terms is often not applied.

The Gartner Group consistently reports that IS/IT projects significantly exceed their time (and cost) estimates. Thus, while almost half of the surveyed firms reported expected implementation expense to be less than $5 million, we consider that figure to still be representative of the minimum scope required. However, recent trends on the part of vendors to reduce implementation time probably have reduced ERP installation cost. Total costs by ERP component are given in Table 2.

Table 2: ERP Installation Project Cost Proportions[4]

Installation Cost Proportion	U.S.	Sweden
Software	30%	24%
Consulting	24%	30%
Hardware	18%	19%
Implementation team	14%	12%
Training	11%	14%
Other	3%	1%

In the U.S., vendors seem to take the biggest chunk of the average implementation. Consultants also take a big portion. These proportions are reversed in Sweden The internal implementation team accounts for an additional 14 percent (12 percent in Sweden). These proportions are roughly reversed in Sweden with training.

Total life cycle costs are needed for evaluation of ERP systems, which have long-range impacts on organizations. Unfortunately, this makes it necessary to estimate costs that are difficult to pin down. Total costs include:[5]

- Software upgrades over time, to include memory and disk space requirements
- Integration, implementation, testing, and maintenance
- Providing users with individual levels of functionality, technical support and service
- Servers
- Disaster recovery and business continuance program
- Electrical service requirements, to include required building modifications
- Staffing.

8.1.1 *Qualitative factors*

While cost is clearly an important matter, there are other factors important in selection of ERP that are difficult to fit into a total cost framework. A survey of European firms in mid-1998 was conducted with the intent of measuring ERP penetration by marke, including questions about criteria for supplier selectiont.[6] There were 2,623 responses for supplier selection criteria. The criteria reportedly used are given in the first column of Table 3, in order of ranking. Product functionality and quality were the criteria most often reported to be important. Column 2 gives related factors reported by Ekanayaka et al. in their framework for evaluating ASPs,[7] while column 3 gives more specifics in that framework.

While these two frameworks don't match entirely, there is a lot of overlap. ASPs would not be expected to have specific impact on the three least important criteria given by Van Everdingen et al. The Ekanayaka et al. framework added two factors important in ASP evaluation: security and service level issues.

8.1.2 *Alternative ERP forms*

The overall ERP selection decision involves the seven broad categories of alternatives shown in Table 4. Each specific organization might generate variants of selected alternatives that suit their particular needs.

Table 3: Selection Evaluation Factors

ERP Supplier Selection (Van Everdingen et al.)	ASP Evaluation (Ekanayaka et al.)	Ekanayaka et al. Subelements
1. Product functionality	Customer service	1. Help desk & training 2. Support for account administration
2. Product quality	Reliability, scalability	
3. Implementation speed	Availability	
4. Interface with other systems	Integration	1. Ability to share data between applications
5. Price	Pricing	1. Effect on total cost structure 2. Hidden costs & charges 3. ROI
6. Market leadership		
7. Corporate image		
8. International orientation		
	Security	1. Physical security of facilities 2. Security of data and applications 3. Back-up and restore procedures 4. Disaster recovery plan
	Service level monitoring & management	1. Clearly defined performance metrics and measurement 2. Defined procedures for opening and closing accounts 3. Flexibility in service offerings, pricing, contract length

Table 4: Alternative ERP Options[8]

Form	Advantages	Disadvantages
In-house	Fit organization	Most difficult, expensive, slowest
In-House + vendor supp.	Blend proven features with organizational fit	Difficult to develop Expensive & slow
Best-of-breed	Theoretically ideal	Hard to link, slow, potentially inefficient
Customize vendor system	Proven features modified to fit organization	Slower, usually more expensive than pure vendor
Select vendor modules	Less risk, fast, inexpensive	If expand, inefficient and higher total cost
Full vendor system	Fast, inexpensive, efficient	Inflexible
ASP	Least risk & cost, fastest	At mercy of ASP

8.2 Multiple Criteria Analysis

Cost-benefit analysis seeks to identify accurate measures of benefits and costs in monetary terms, and uses the ratio benefits/costs (the term benefit-cost ratio seems more appropriate, and is sometimes used, but most people refer to cost-benefit analysis). Because ERP projects involve long time frames (for benefits if not for costs as well), considering the net present value of benefits and costs is important.

Recognition that real life decisions involve high levels of uncertainty is reflected in the development of fuzzy multiattribute models. The basic multiattribute model is to maximize value as a function of importance and performance:

$$value_j = \sum_{i=1}^{K} w_i \times u(x_{ij}) \qquad (1)$$

where w_i is the weight of attribute i, K is the number of attributes, and $u(x_{ij})$ is the score of alternative x_j on attribute i.

Multiple criteria analysis considers benefits on a variety of scales without directly converting them to some common scale such as dollars.[9]

The method (there are many variants of multiple criteria analysis) is not at all perfect. But it does provide a way to demonstrate to decision makers the relative positive and negative features of alternatives, and gives a way to quantify the preferences of decision makers.

We will consider an analysis of five alternative forms of ERP: a system built in-house, a best-of-breed system, a vendor system customized to provide functionality unique to the organization, a vendor system without customization, and an ASP. We will make a leap to assume that complete total life cycle costs have been estimated for each option as given in Table 5.

Table 5: Total Life Cycle Costs for Each Option ($ million)

Option	Soft ware	Consultants	Hard ware	Implement	Train	Total Cost
A: Vendor A	15	6	6	5	8	40
B: Vendor B	12	9	6	6	9	42
C: A Customized	13	8	6	10	2	39
D: Best-of-Breed	16	12	6	9	11	54
E: ASP	3	4	0	2	8	17

The greatest software cost is expected to be for the best-of-breed option, while the ASP would have a major advantage. The best-of-breed option is expected to have the highest consulting cost, with ASP again having a relative advantage. Hardware is the same for the first four options, with the ASP option saving a great deal. Implementation is expected to be highest for the customized system, with ASP having an advantage. Training is lowest for the customized system, while the best-of-breed system the highest.

But there are other important factors as well. This total cost estimate assumes that everything will go as planned, and may not consider other qualitative aspects. Multiple criteria analysis provides the ability to incorporate other factors.

Perhaps the easiest application of multiple criteria analysis is the simple multiattribute rating theory (SMART) identifies the relative importance of criteria in terms of weights, and measures the relative performance of each alternative on each criterion in terms of scores.[10]

In this application, we will include criteria from Ekanayaka et al.[11] of:

- Customer service
- Reliability, availability, scalability
- Integration
- Financial factors
- Security
- Service level monitoring and management

The relative importance is given by the order, following Van Everdingen et al.[12]

8.2.1 *Scores*

Scores in SMART can be used to convert performances (subjective or objective) to a zero-one scale, where zero represents the worst acceptable performance level in the mind of the decision maker, and one represents the ideal, or possibly the best performance desired. Note that these ratings are subjective, a function of individual preference. Scores for the criteria given in the value analysis example could be as in Table 6:

Table 6: Relative Scores by Criteria for Each Option in Example

Option	Customer Service	Reliability, Availability, Scalability	Integra-tion	Cost	Security	Service Level
A: Vendor A	0.8	1	0.9	0.6	1	0.9
B: Vendor B	0.6	0.7	1	0.5	0.9	1
C: A Customized	0.9	0.5	0.8	0.8	0.7	0.8
D: Best-of-Breed	1	0.6	0.6	0.2	0.6	0.6
E: ASP	0.5	0	0.7	1	0	1

The best imaginable customer service level would be provided by the best-of-breed option. The ASP option is considered suspect on this factor, but not the worst imaginable. The Vendor A system without customization is expected to be the most reliable, while the ASP option the worst. The Vendor B option is rated the easiest to integrate. The ASP and best-of-breed systems are rated low on this factor, but not the worst imaginable. Costs reflect Table 5, converting dollar estimates into value scores on the 0-1 scale. The ASP option has the best imaginable cost. The Vendor A system without customization is rated as the best possible with respect to security issues, while the ASP is rated the worst possible. Service level ratings are high for the Vendor Br system and the ASP, while the best-of-breed system is rated low on this factor.

8.2.2 *Weights*

The next phase of the analysis ties these ratings together into an overall value function by obtaining the relative weight of each criterion. In order to give the decision maker a reference about what exactly is being compared, the relative range between best and worst on each scale for each criterion should be explained. There are many methods to determine these weights. In SMART, the process begins with rank-ordering the four criteria. A possible ranking for a specific decision maker might be as given in Table 7.

Table 7: Worst and Best Measures by Criteria

Criteria	Worst Measure	Best Measure
Customer service	0.5 – ASP	1 – Best-of-Breed
Reliability, Availability, Scalability	0 – ASP	1 – Vendor A
Integration	0.6 – Best-of-Breed	1 – Vendor B
Cost	0.2 – Best-of-breed	1 – ASP
Security	0 – ASP	1 – Vendor A
Service level	0.6 – Best-of-Breed	1 – Vendor B & ASP

Swing weighting could be used to identify weights.[13] Here, the scoring was used to reflect 1 as the best possible and 0 as the worst imaginable. Thus the relative rank ordering reflects a common scale, and can be used directly in the order given (which was based on the Van Everdingen et al. survey).[14] To obtain relative criterion weights, the first step is to rank-order criteria by importance. Two estimates of weights can be obtained. The first assigns the least important criterion 10 points, and assesses the relative importance of each of the other criteria on that basis. This process (including rank-ordering and assigning relative values based upon moving from worst measure to best measure based on most important criterion) is demonstrated in Table 8.

Table 8: Weight Estimation from Perspective of Most Important Criterion

Criteria	Worst Measure	Best Measure	Assigned Value
1-Customer service	0	1	100
2-Reliability, Availability, Scalability	0	1	80
3-Integration	0	1	50
4-Cost	0	1	20
5-Security	0	1	10
6-Service level	0	1	5

The total of the assigned values is 265. One estimate of relative weights is obtained by dividing each assigned value by 265. Before we do that, we obtain a second estimate from the perspective of the least important criterion, which is assigned a value of 10 as in Table 9.

Table 9: Weight Estimation from Perspective of Least Important Criterion

Criteria	Worst Measure	Best Measure	Assigned Value
6-Service level	0	1	10
5-Security	0	1	25
4-Cost	0	1	50
3-Integration	0	1	90
2-Reliability, Availability, Scalability	0	1	150
1-Customer service	0	1	200

These add up to 525. The two weight estimates are now as shown in Table 10.

Table 10: Criterion Weight Development

Criteria	Based on Best		Based on Worst		Compromise
1-Customer service	100/265	0.377	200/525	0.381	**0.38**
2-Reliability, Availability, Scalability	80/265	0.302	150/525	0.286	**0.30**
3-Integration	50/265	0.189	90/525	0.171	**0.18**
4-Cost	20/265	0.075	50/525	0.095	**0.08**
5-Security	10/265	0.038	25/525	0.048	**0.04**
6-Service level	5/265	0.019	10/525	0.019	**0.02**

The last criterion can be used to make sure that the sum of compromise weights adds up to 1.00.

8.2.3 *Value score*

The next step of the SMART method is to obtain value scores for each alternative by multiplying each score on each criterion for an alternative by that criterion's weight, and adding these products by alternative. Table 11 shows this calculation.

Table 11: Value Score Calculation

Criteria	Wgt	Vendor A	Vendor B	Customize	Best-of-B	ASP
Customer service	**0.38**	× 0.8 = 0.304	× 0.6 = 0.228	× 0.9 = 0.342	× 1.0 = 0.380	× 0.5 = 0.190
Reliability, Avail, Scalable	**0.30**	× 1.0 = 0.300	× 0.7 = 0.210	× 0.5 = 0.150	× 0.6 = 0.180	× 0 = 0.000
Integration	**0.18**	× 0.9 = 0.162	× 1.0 = 0.180	× 0.8 = 0.144	× 0.6 = 0.108	× 0.7 = 0.126
Cost	**0.08**	× 0.6 = 0.048	× 0.5 = 0.040	× 0.8 = 0.064	× 0.2 = 0.016	× 1.0 = 0.080
Security	**0.04**	× 1.0 = 0.040	× 0.9 = 0.036	× 0.7 = 0.028	× 0.6 = 0.024	× 0.0 = 0.000
Service level	**0.02**	× 0.9 = 0.018	× 1.0 = 0.020	× 0.8 = 0.016	× 0.6 = 0.012	× 1.0 = 0.020
TOTALS		0.872	0.714	0.744	0.720	0.416

In this example, the ASP turned out to be quite unattractive, even though it had the best cost and the best service level. The cost advantage was outweighed by this option's poor ratings on customer service levels expected, reliability, availability, and scalability, and security, two of which were the highest rated criteria. The value score indicates that the uncustomized Vendor A system would be best, followed by the customized system and Vendor B's system.

8.2.4 *Other multiple criteria methods*

There are many other approaches implementing roughly the same idea. The best known is multiattribute utility theory, which uses more sophisticated (but not necessarily more accurate) methods to obtain both scores and weights. The analytic hierarchy process is another well-known approach.[15]

8.3 Conclusions

Outsourcing ERP is a very important issue. ASPs have recently become major players in this market. While some forms of outsourcing on a large scale have been around for over a decade, in the past outsourcing was done through major software firms acting as service consultants, 8such as EDS.

Outsourcing in its current form introduces a number of important issues. While the cost of outsourcing is expected to be much lower, paradoxically it could lead to very high costs if things go wrong. The total life cycle cost estimated is quite unpredictabile. ASPs also offer lower risk with respect to the vendor market, but again paradoxically involve the highest risk with respect to ASP survival. Meaningful and accurate cost benefit ratios in this environment are very hard to implement. Multiple criteria analysis offers a way to incorporate less quantified factors into rational decision models.

Endnotes

1. Bryson, K.M., Sullivan, W.E. (2003). Designing effective incentive-oriented contracts for application service provider hosting of ERP systems. *Business Process Management Journal* 9:6 705-721.
2. Bryson and Sullivan (2003), op cit. ; . Clymer, J. (2004). Rent or buy? *PC Magazine* 23:18 129-132, 136, 138 (October 19); ___, (2003). ERP outsourcing. *CIO Insight* 27, 72 (June).
3. Olson, D.L. (2004). *Managerial Issues of Enterprise Resource Planning Systems*. Boston: McGraw-Hill/Irwin.
4. Extracted from Mabert, V.M., Soni, A., Venkataramanan, M.A. (2000). Enterprise resource planning survey of US manufacturing firms. *Production and Inventory Management Journal* 41:20, 52-58; Olhager, J., Selldin, E. (2003). Enterprise resource planning survey of Swedish manufacturing firms. *European Journal of Operational Research* 146, 365-373.
5. McCarthy, T. (2001). Are ASPs for you? *Financial Executive* **17**:4, 45-48 (June).
6. Van Everdingen, Y., van Hellegersberg, J., Waarts, E. (2000). ERP adoption by European midsize companies, *Communications of the ACM* 43:4, 27-31.
7. Ekanayaka, Y., Currie, W.L., Seltsikas, P. (2003). Evaluating application service providers. *Benchmarking: An International Journal* **10**:4, 343-354.
8. Olson (2004), op cit.
9. Keeney, R.L., Raiffa, H., (1976). *Decisions with Multiple Objectives: Preferences and Value Tradeoffs* (New York: John Wiley & Sons); Olson, D.L. (1996). *Decision Aids for Selection Problems* (New York: Springer); Hobbs, B.F., Horn, G.T.F. (1997). Building public confidence in energy planning: A multimethod MCDM approach to demand-side planning at BC Gas. *Energy Policy* 25:3, 356-375.
10. Edwards, W. (1977). How to use multiattribute utility measurement for social decisionmaking. *IEEE Transactions on Systems, Man, and Cybernetics* SMC-7:5, 326-340.

11. Ekankaya et al. (2003), op cit.
12. Van Everdingen et al. (2000), op cit.
13. Edwards (1977), op cit.
14. Van Everdingen et al. (2000), op cit.
15. Saaty, T.L. (1977). A scaling method for priorities in hierarchical structures. *Journal of Mathematical Psychology* 15 234-281.

Chapter 9

Simulation and DEA Models of Risk

> Describes supply chain operations
> Reviews primary risks involved in supply chains
> Describes a supply chain vendor selection decision
> Presents a multiple objective programming model for this decision
> Presents a data envelopment analysis (DEA) model for this decision
> Discusses the application of simulation to analyze probabilistic
>   aspects of the decision

Supply chains are connections of organizations (or possible single organizational elements, as in 19th Century vertically integrated systems) connecting raw materials with customers. One of their most impressive modern manifestations is in the form of mammoth retail establishments such as Wal-Mart or Carrefours. In this form, the goods of the world are tapped to be delivered to hundreds of millions of customers in widespread retail outlets. Supply chain participants can include manufacturers at low cost locations such as China, India, or Vietnam, assemblers at high-tech operations in Taiwan and Korea, and distributors where customers reside all over the globe. They can also include e-business operations such as Amazon.com.

Supply chains are networks of suppliers/vendors, manufacturers, distributors, and retailers that are connected by transportation, information, and financial infrastructure.[1] The ability to specialize and coordinate through e-business has led to complex supply chains that seem to develop from markets rather than the plans of specific organizations.[2] Current supply chain technology includes potentially many suppliers/vendors linked to one or more manufacturers and/or assemblers, who often use multiple distributors to supply many retailers. Industry supply chain leaders such as i2 and Manugistics have developed tools to share sales and forecast data, and enterprise resource planning software often features such support.[3]

Supply chains need to provide an adequate service level (minimizing stock-out costs) while controlling overall costs of holding, ordering, transporting, and purchasing. The more permanent relationships found in supply chains often include lower purchasing costs for the core supply chain member, which may pass these savings on to customers (another form of better service). If the vendor (or supplier) has more complete information about demand, they might more efficiently manage their operations. Furthermore, the dynamic environment in 21st Century retail and service makes it necessary to keep up with rapid changes in demands, which can complicate holding costs. Four hidden costs of inventory can be present in supply chains:[4]

1. Component devaluation costs – short life value of items or components;
2. Price protection costs – if discounts are offered, prior distributors may need to be reimbursed at to the same price level;
3. Product return costs – distributors could return unsold goods for full refund;
4. Obsolescence costs – product outdating.

A common occurrence in 21st Century business is outsourcing product manufacturing. This usually is motivated by lower product costs. There are increased risks expected from differences in product quality, as well as differences in the probabilities of late delivery. Many other factors have been considered as well.[5] Another risk-reducing strategy is to rely upon long-term commitments. Selection of supply chain partners is an important decision involving many important factors.

Various models are available to select supply chain partners in existing literatures, taking into consideration of uncertainty and risk. Most researchers propose to derive the probability distribution from historical data and model the SC uncertainty (e.g., uncertain demand) using the derived probability distributions in a decision model.[6]

However, these decision models may result in sub-optimal solutions since they typically consider one objective function, e.g., the minimization of expected cost or maximization of expected profit. Multiple criteria are quite often in deciding on selecting supply chain partners and sourcing arrangements.[7] These researches seldom simultaneously consider multiple objective and uncertainty and risk. Simulation-based optimization may provide an alternative approach for dealing with the SC risk and uncertainty.

This chapter considers three types of vendor selection models in supply chains with risk: the multi-objective programming model (MOP), Data envelopment analysis (DEA) and Chance constrained programming (CCP). Using assumed probability distribution in risk-embedded attributes, we run three types of simulation-based optimization models: a Monte Carlo simulation to chance constrained programs, simulation to MOP and DEA simulation.

We model a supply chain consisting of three levels and use simulated data with distributions empirically derived. Results from three models as well as simulation models are compared and a comprehensive analysis is carried out.

9.1 Supply Chain Risk

Supply chain operations involve many opportunities to gain the benefits of trade. But they also involve risks. Trade has historically involved risks of shipping, one of the primary motivations for the early insurance industry. Most transportation risks have been brought under control (although piracy still exists, and ships still sink, if only occasionally). But many supply chain risks have been identified. Ojala and Hallikas analyzed supplier investment risks, and how each could be managed.[8] Li modeled supplier risk attitude with respect to risk aversion.[9]

9.1.1 *Supply chain models*

A variety of models have been resented to aid decision making in supply chains under conditions of risk. Barbarosoğlu and Yazgaç applied an AHP model to a set of 72 criteria in categories involving strategic partnership, business and manufacturing performance, and supply chain management.[10] Other models have considered multiple criteria.[11] Others have combined fuzzy data with genetic algorithms,[12] or bicriterion mathematical programming model for supply chain inventory.[13]

This chapter considers three types of risk evaluation models within supply chains. Data envelopment analysis (DEA) provides a means to evaluate relative efficiency of multiple criteria mathematical programming models. DEA has been used in supply chains[14] and in vendor selection.[15] Chance constrained programming (CCP) allows used of probabilistic constraints within mathematical programming models, and has been applied to supply chain coordination decisions.[16] Multi-objective programming models (MOP) aim to select preferred vendor by considering the tradeoff of various objectives, e.g., cost minimization, quick response and timely delivery.

9.1.2 *Supply chain risk model*

We model a supply chain consisting of three levels: a set of ten suppliers, six domestic and four international, each with expected costs, quality acceptance levels, and on-time delivery distributions. Distributions of costs are assumed normal, distributions of acceptance failure are assumed exponential and distributions of late delivery are assumed lognormal. These represent assumptions that could be replaced by distributions empirically derived. The core level represents the organizing, decision-making retail system. The third level is represented by twenty customers, each with a demand assumed to be normal for a given period. The retailer must anticipate demand and order quantities of the modeled good to be delivered to arrive on time at each demand destination. Profit is gained from sales made for goods successfully delivered to each demand. Revenue is assumed at $2 per item sold. Costs are probabilistic as outlined above, but total cost of goods sold has a mean given for each source supplier. Goods not passing quality acceptance level are not paid for. Goods delivered late are paid for at a reduced rate, and are carried forward at an inventory cost. Table 1 provides data for the supply chain model vendors.

Table 1: Vendor Data

Vendor	Unit Cost	Accept Rate	On-time Rate	Maximum
V1	1.00 (0.01)	0.999	0.98 (0.03)	10000
V2	0.95 (0.02)	0.995	0.97 (0.03)	10000
V3	0.98 (0.03)	0.99	0.97 (0.03)	9000
V4	1.03 (0.01)	0.98	0.98 (0.03)	8000
V5	1.05 (0.05)	0.97	0.96 (0.03)	8000
V6	1.1 (0.03)	0.95	0.97 (0.03)	7000
V7	0.75 (0.05)	0.98	0.90 (0.03)	10000
V8	0.60 (0.06)	0.95	0.88 (0.03)	8000
V9	0.55 (0.07)	0.90	0.86 (0.03)	6000
V10	0.50 (0.08)	0.80	0.85 (0.03)	4000

Data given is means (standard deviation); Unit costs normally distributed, Accept rate exponentially distributed, on-time rate lognormally distributed.

Table 2: Demand Data

Demand	Average (std)	Minimum Per Period
D1	3000 (300)	1000
D2	2800 (300)	1000
D3	2200 (300)	1000
D4	1800 (300)	1000
D5	1500 (300)	500
D6	1300 (300)	500
D7	1200 (250)	500
D8	1200 (250)	500
D9	1200 (250)	400
D10	1100 (250)	300
D11	1100 (250)	200
D12	1100 (200)	100
D13	800 (200)	0
D14	700 (150)	0
D15	500 (150)	0
D16	300 (100)	0
D17	300 (100)	0
D18	200 (100)	0
D19	200 (50)	0
D20	200 (50)	0

Twenty demand sites are modeled, each seeking one common product. Product price is $2 per item, time period assumed is a week. Different conditions could be modeled with little difficulty other than scale.

9.1.3 *Multi-objective programming model*

Notations in the multi-objective programming model are defined as follows:

n_i = the number of candidate suppliers desired by the ith customer.

x_{ij} = decision variables, quantity purchased by the ith customer from supplier j.

z_{ij} = decision variables = $\begin{cases} 1, & \text{if if supplier j is selected by the } i^{th} \text{ customer,} \\ 0, & \text{otherwise.} \end{cases}$

c_{ij} = per unit purchase cost from supplier j by the ith customer.

λ_{ij} = percentage of items late from supplier j to the ith customer.

β_{ij} = percentage of rejected units from supplier j.

D = total demand for the item.

D_i = demand for item over planning period from the ith customer.

u_{ij}^{u} = maximum amount of business for item to be given to supplier j by the ith customer.

u_{ij}^{l} = minimum amount of business for item to be given to supplier j by the ith customer.

w_{ij}^{u} = maximum order quantity from supplier j by the ith customer.

w_{ij}^{l} = minimum order quantity from supplier j by the ith customer.

Objectives and constraints are defined as follows:

Objective 1: Minimize the total purchase cost.
Objective 2: Minimize the number of or rejected items.
Objective 3: Minimize the number of late deliveries.
Constraint 4: Ensures that the quantity demand is met.
Constraint 5: Ensures that the vendor's capacity is not exceeded.
Constraint 6: Ensures that the customer's proposed business to the vendor is not exceeded.

Constraint 7: Establishes minimum order quantities the vendors supply.
Constraint 8: Establishes minimum business for selected vendors.
Constraint 9: Ensures that there are no negative orders.
Constraint 10: Establishes binary nature of vendor selection decision.

First we present the multi-objective programming model suggested below. This model differs from other models in that it considers different demand risk from many different customers. We only consider a single assembler, who has only one attribute, i.e., demand.

$$\text{Min} \quad f_1(x_{ij}) = \sum_{i=1}^{m} \sum_{j=1}^{n_i} c_{ij} x_{ij} \quad \{\text{total cost}\} \tag{9-1}$$

$$\text{Min} \quad f_2(x_{ij}) = \sum_{i=1}^{m} \sum_{j=1}^{n_i} \beta_{ij} x_{ij} \quad \{\text{\# rejected}\} \tag{9-2}$$

$$\text{Min} \quad f_3(x_{ij}) = \sum_{i=1}^{m} \sum_{j=1}^{n_i} \lambda_{ij} x_{ij} \quad \{\text{\# late}\} \tag{9-3}$$

subject to:

$$\sum_j x_{ij} \geq D_i, \, \mathbf{i} = 1, \ldots, \mathbf{m} \tag{9-4}$$

$$x_{ij} \geq z_{ij} u_{ij}^l, \, \forall \, \text{i,j} \tag{9-5}$$

$$x_{ij} \leq z_{ij} u_{ij}^u \, \{\text{lower and upper bounds}\}, \, \forall \, \text{i,j} \tag{9-6}$$

$$x_{ij} \geq z_{ij} w_{ij}^l, \, \forall \, \text{i,j} \tag{9-7}$$

$$x_{ij} \leq z_{ij} w_{ij}^u \, \{\text{lower and upper order bounds}\}, \, \forall \, \text{i,j} \tag{9-8}$$

$$\sum_j z_{ij} = n_i, \, \{\text{\# of vendors satisfy desired number}\} \tag{9-9}$$

$$x_{ij} \geq 0 \tag{9-10}$$

$$z_{ij} = \{0,1\}, \, \forall \, \text{i,j} \tag{9-11}$$

where $j = 1, \ldots, n_i$, represents the possible vendors selected for the ith customer.

This model simultaneously minimizes the purchase cost ($f_1(x_{ij})$), percentage of items delivered late ($f_2(x_{ij})$) and percentage of items rejected ($f_3(x_{ij})$), while meeting various constraints e.g. with respect to minimum and maximum order quantities. These goals were also used in a multicriteria mathematical programming supply chain model.[17] We have lower and upper bound for x_{ij} from both the vendor and the customer's point of view, as expressed in Constraint (5) (6) (7) and (8). It is not obvious how to treat the various goals.[18] For example, the goals might be minimized sequentially or weights might be introduced making it a single criterion search problem, much as the weighted sum of various objectives approach or goal programming approach.[19]

A standard technique for MOP is to minimize a positively weighted convex sum of the objectives, that is, $\operatorname{Min} \Sigma_q \omega_q f_q(x_{ij})$, where the weights of three objectives can be expressed by ($\omega_1, \omega_2, \omega_3$) with $\Sigma \omega_q = 1$, q = 1,...3, $0 < \omega_q < 1$. It is easy to prove that the minimum of this combined function is Pareto optimal. It is up to the user to choose appropriate weights. Though computationally more expensive, this approach gives an idea of the shape of the Pareto surface and provides the user with more information about the trade-off among the various objectives. In order to examine the customer's preference over different objectives, three scenarios are analyzed in terms of weight attached to three objectives: ($\omega_1, \omega_2, \omega_3$) = (0.6, 0.2, 0.2), ($\omega_1, \omega_2, \omega_3$) = (0.2, 0.6, 0.2) and ($\omega_1, \omega_2, \omega_3$) = (0.2, 0.2, 0.6). This scenario analysis is necessary since the buyer's procurement priorities tend to shift from quality and delivery performance (($\omega_1, \omega_2, \omega_3$) = (0.2, 0.6, 0.2) and ($\omega_1, \omega_2, \omega_3$) = (0.2, 0.2, 0.6)) to cost minimization (($\omega_1, \omega_2, \omega_3$) = (0.6, 0.2, 0.2)), particularly in a case product life cycle is taken into consideration[20]. Table 3 presents supplier selected and order quantity from MOP models. As can be seen from Table 3, the buyer's selecting of suppliers and ordering quantity change as his preference over different objectives changes. Interestingly enough, when the weight attached to cost objective is larger, the buyer tends to choose V7, V8, V9 and V10, which can provides lower unit cost than the rest. Those providing high unit cost, i.e., V1-V3, V5 and V6 are never selected by any customer. Moreover, for the two selected suppliers, the customer prefer to order more from the supplier providing lower unit cost than from the one providing higher unit cost. For example, as shown in the second and third row of Table 3, both D1 and D2 selected V10 and V9. Both D1 and D2 order more from V10 than from V9 since V10 provides an average unit cost 0.5, which is lower than 0.55 by V9.

As the buyer's procurement priorities shift from cost minimization to quality and delivery performance, V1 and V2, which can provides high quality and delivery performance, are more preferred by the buyer. Those providing poor quality and delivery performance, e.g., V10 are unlikely to be selected.

Table 3: Supplier Selected and Order Quantity from MOP

	$(\omega_1, \omega_2, \omega_3) =$ (0.6, 0.2, 0.2)				$(\omega_1, \omega_2, \omega_3) =$ (0.2, 0.6, 0.2)				$(\omega_1, \omega_2, \omega_3) =$ (0.2, 0.2, 0.6)			
	Supplier selected		Order quantity		Supplier selected		Order quantity		Supplier selected		Order quantity	
D1	10	9	2000	1000	8	7	2000	1000	8	2	2000	1000
D2	10	9	1800	1000	8	7	1800	1000	8	2	1800	1000
D3	9	8	1200	1000	8	7	1200	1000	8	2	1200	1000
D4	9	8	1000	1000	8	7	1000	1000	8	2	1000	1000
D5	9	8	1000	500	8	7	1000	500	8	2	1000	500
D6	9	8	800	500	8	7	800	500	8	2	800	500
D7	8	7	700	500	9	7	500	700	2	1	700	500
D8	8	7	700	500	9	7	500	700	2	1	700	500
D9	8	7	800	400	9	7	400	800	2	1	800	400
D10	8	7	800	300	9	7	300	800	2	1	800	300
D11	10	8	200	900	9	7	200	900	2	1	900	200
D12	8	7	1000	100	8	7	200	900	8	2	200	900
D13	8	7	100	700	9	7	600	200	2	1	200	600
D14	7	4	699	1	9	2	697	3	9	1	2	698
D15	7	4	499	1	9	2	497	3	1	9	498	2
D16	7	4	299	1	9	2	297	3	9	1	2	298
D17	7	4	299	1	9	2	297	3	9	1	2	298
D18	7	4	199	1	9	2	197	3	9	1	2	198
D19	7	4	199	1	2	9	3	197	9	1	2	198
D20	7	4	199	1	9	2	197	3	9	1	2	198

9.1.4 *Chance constrained model*

This section uses chance constrained programs to model a simplified case: a three-level supply chain with only one customer.

Two types of models are used here. One is used to generate orders from suppliers using mathematical programming. A chance constrained model is considered to model the highest level of complexity assumed (recognizing that any model leaves out some details). Simplified linear programming models are used to generate solutions.

1) Maximization of expected cost, considering expected losses from acceptance inspection or late delivery.
2) The same objective considering only the first six variables, representing domestic suppliers only.

Minimization of expected cost adjusted for expected loss rates with constraints added to provide buffers for service level (considering quality acceptance and late delivery). This simplification technique is similar to the goal programming approach where we minimize one objective while constraining the remaining objectives to be less than given target values. This method is especially useful if the user can afford to solve just one optimization problem. However, it is not always easy to choose appropriate "goals" for the constraints. Thus, constraint level combinations of 0.90, 0.95, and 0.99 (translating to normal z-functions of 1.28, 1.64, and 1.96) for both acceptance and on-time delivery were used, resulting in three additional models. Solutions obtained are given in Table 2:

Table 4: Decisions Obtained from CCP

Ordered	Base	Domestic	At 0.9	At 0.95	At 0.99
V1	0	4500	0	0	0
V2	0	10000	1157	1536	2246
V3	0	9000	0	0	0
V4	0	0	0	0	0
V5	0	0	0	0	0
V6	0	0	0	0	0
V7	9805	0	10000	10000	10000
V8	8000	0	8000	8000	8000
V9	6000	0	6000	6000	6000
V10	4000	0	4000	4000	4000

Vendors selected by CCP fits those by MOP model in Section 2.2.1. V2, V7-10 are frequently selected by both CCP and MOP. V4, V5 and V6 are never selected by CCP and V5 and V6 are never selected by MOP.

9.1.5 *DEA model*

DEA can be used for a comparison and constitutes a useful complement to the available decision models for supplier selection. We present in the Appendix the basics of DEA. Each DEA seeks to determine which of the n candidate vendors define an envelopment surface that represents best practice, referred to as the efficient frontier. Units that lie on the surface are deemed efficient in DEA while those units that do not, are termed inefficient. DEA provides a comprehensive analysis of relative efficiencies for multiple input-multiple output situations by evaluating each vendor and measuring its performance relative to an envelopment surface composed of other vendors. DEA "scans" the available suppliers and identifies the efficient subset of suppliers. Those vendors known as the efficient reference set are the peer group for the inefficient units. Thus, a DEA model can serve as a 'filter' before the determination of final selected suppliers. Various DEA models are available and many model extensions can be used to provide a more comprehensive review of candidate vendor performance. For example, we can use categorical variables such as the competitive environment and vendor location to enhance the model and add additional variables to either model if more vendors become available for study. We can also add weight restrictions to the models to refine the results and lead to more realistic recommended improvements. We will develop DEA simulation models to implement some extensions while keep others as further considerations.

9.2 Simulation

Simulation models are sets of assumptions concerning the relationship among model components. Simulations can be time-oriented (for instance, involving the number of events such as demands in a day) or process-oriented (for instance, involving queuing systems of arrivals and services). Uncertainty can be included by using probabilistic inputs for elements such as demands, inter-arrival times, or service times. These probabilistic inputs need to be described by probability distributions with specified parameters. Probability distributions can include normal distributions (with parameters for mean and variance), exponential distributions (with parameter for a mean), lognormal (parameters mean and variance), or any of a number of other distributions. A simulation run is a sample from an infinite population of possible results for a given model. After a simulation model is built, a selected number of trials is established. Statistical methods are used to validate simulation models and design simulation experiments.

Many financial simulation models can be accomplished on spreadsheets, such as Excel. There are a number of commercial add-on products that can be added to Excel, such as @Risk or Crystal Ball, that vastly extend the simulation power of spreadsheet models.[21] These add-ons make it very easy to replicate simulation runs, and include the ability to correlate variables, expeditiously select from standard distributions, aggregate and display output, and other useful functions.

9.2.1 *The simulation process*

Using simulation effectively requires careful attention to the modeling and implementation process. The simulation process consists of five essential steps:

1. **Develop a conceptual model of the system or problem under study.** This step begins with understanding and defining the problem, identifying the goals and objectives of the study, determining the important input variables, and defining output measures. It might also include a detailed logical description of the system that is being studied. Simulation models should be made as simple as possible to focus on critical factors that make a difference in the decision. The cardinal rule of modeling is to build simple models first, then embellish and enrich them as necessary.

2. **Build the simulation model.** This includes developing appropriate formulas or equations, collecting any necessary data, determining the probability distributions of uncertain variables, and constructing a format for recording the results. This might entail designing a spreadsheet, developing a computer program, or formulating the model according to the syntax of a special computer simulation language (which we discuss further in Chapter 7).

3. **Verify and validate the model.** Verification refers to the process of ensuring that the model is free from logical errors; that is, that it does what it is intended to do. Validation ensures that it is a reasonable representation of the actual system or problem. These are important steps to lend credibility to simulation models and gain acceptance from managers and other users. These approaches are described further in the next section.

4. **Design experiments using the model.** This step entails determining the values of the controllable variables to be studied or the questions to be answered in order to address the decision maker's objectives.

5. **Perform the experiments and analyze the results.** Run the appropriate simulations to obtain the information required to make an informed decision.

As with any modeling effort, this approach is not necessarily serial. Often, you must return to pervious steps as new information arises or as results suggest modifications to the model. Therefore, simulation is an evolutionary process that must involve not only analysts and model developers, but also the users of the results.

9.2.2 *Cash management simulation*

The *Miller-Orr model* in finance addresses the problem of managing its cash position by purchasing or selling securities at a transaction cost in order to lower or raise its cash position. That is, the firm needs to have enough cash on hand to meet its obligations, but does not want to maintain too high a cash balance because it loses the opportunity for earning higher interest by investing in other securities. The Miller-Orr model assumes that the firm will maintain a minimum cash balance, m, a maximum cash balance, M, and an ideal level, R, called the return point. Cash is managed using a decision rule that states that whenever the cash balance falls to m, R - m securities are sold to bring the balance up to the return point. When the cash balance rises to M, M - R securities are purchased to reduce the cash balance back to the return point. Using some advanced mathematics, the return point and maximum cash balance levels are shown to be:

$$R = m + Z \qquad\qquad (9\text{-}12)$$

$$M = R + 2Z$$

where

$$Z = \left(\frac{3C_0 \sigma^2}{4r} \right)^{1/3}$$

σ^2 = variance of the daily cash flows, and
r = average daily rate of return corresponding to the premium associated with securities.

For example, if the premium is 4%, r = .04/365. To apply the model, note that we do not need to know the actual demand for cash, only the daily variance. Essentially, the Miller-Orr model determines the decision rule that minimizes the expected costs of making the cash-security transactions and the expected opportunity costs of maintaining the cash balance based on the variance of the cash requirements.

Figure 1 shows a spreadsheet for implementing the model and for simulating the results. In the simulation model, we begin with a cash level equal to the return point. The next day's requirement is randomly generated in column C as a normal random variate with mean 0 and variance given in cell D5. The decision rule is applied in column D. If the cash balance for the current day (cell B13) is less than or equal to the minimum level (cell D6), we sell D8-B13 dollars of securities to bring the balance up to the return point. Otherwise, if the cash balance exceeds the upper limit (D9), we buy enough securities (i.e. subtract an amount of cash) to bring the balance back down to the return point. If neither of these conditions hold, there is no transaction and the balance for the next day is simply the current value plus the net requirement.

	A	B	C	D
1			Miller-Orr Model Inputs	
2				
3			Transaction cost	35
4			Interest rate premium of securities	0.04
5			Variance of daily cash flows	60000
6			Required minimum balance	7500
7				
8			Return point	=D6+(3*D3*D5/(4*D4/365))^(1/3)
9			Upper limit	=D8+2*(3*D3*D5/(4*D4/365))^(1/3)
10				
11			Next Day	Transaction
12	Day	Cash	Required	Amount
13	0	=D8	=NORMINV(RAND(),0, SQRT($D$5))	0
14	1	=B13 +C13 +D13	=NORMINV(RAND(),0, SQRT($D$5))	=IF(B14<=$D$6,$D$8-B14,IF(B14>=$D$9,-B14+$D$8,0))
15	2	=B14 +C14 +D14	=NORMINV(RAND(),0, SQRT($D$5))	=IF(B15<=$D$6,$D$8-B15,IF(B15>=$D$9,-B15+$D$8,0))

Figure 1: Miller Orr Spreadsheet Model in Excel

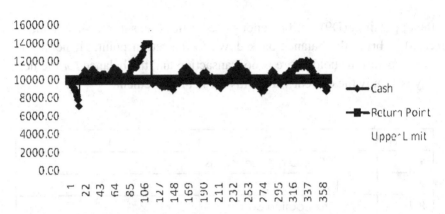

Figure 2: Miller-Orr Excel Model Output for One Year

9.2.3 *Risk management simulation models*

This section presents three simulation models: a Monte Carlo simulation to chance constrained programs, DEA simulation and simulation to MOP. Monte Carlo simulation to chance constrained programs generates quite consistent result as DEA simulation does. Simulation to MOP considers risks across various customers, which is a more complicated situation than that in the former two models.

Monte Carlo Simulation and Chance Constrained Programming

Using Excel and Crystal Ball, the five ordering plans were used with the assumed distributions, calculating expected profit, end of period excess or shortage, rejected items, and late items. Profit was calculated as $2 times the minimum of items purchased by policy minus rejected or late items, and sum of customer demand, less $0.01 per excess item to reflect inventory carrying cost. The simulation was implemented in Crystal Ball, an Excel add-on, which provides means to easily generate probability distributions. Each vendor had three probabilistic elements: cost, acceptance, and on-time delivery, as given earlier. To control for random differences across policies, the outcomes (profit, rejections, late deliveries) were applied to each of the five policies in each model. One thousand runs were conducted.

Table 5: Simulation Means

	Base	Domestic	At 0.9	At 0.95	At 0.99
Profit	23864	15166	24778	25027	25494
Excess	225	15166	339	370	441
Short	8373	7861	7638	7428	7047
Rejects	9968	7814	10405	10527	10756
Late	3302	827	3368	3384	3413
Service level	0.63	0.66	0.67	0.67	0.69

DEA simulation

To investigate and illustrate the performance of the candidate vendors and compare the results to those from other models, we have carried out three simulations: 200 simulation runs and 1000 simulation runs. Input and output data are randomly generated using the assumed distributions in each of these simulation runs. We estimate the DEA efficiency score given to each vendor of interests each time we run DEA. We finally calculate the average DEA efficiency scores and standard deviation in the total runs. Table 6 presents the average efficiency score, standard derivation, the 95 percent of confidence interval for the mean and the percentage (number) of efficient DMUs in the stochastic DEA simulation models.

Table 6: Computation from DEA simulation Models

Vendor	200 simulation runs				1500 simulation runs			
	Mean	STD	CL(95.0%)	#efficient	Mean	STD	CL(95.0%)	#efficient
V1	0.618	0.138	0.02	9	0.621	0.151	0.008	115
V2	0.642	0.148	0.02	19	0.636	0.146	0.007	109
V3	0.621	0.147	0.02	12	0.622	0.146	0.007	96
V4	0.618	0.163	0.02	13	0.596	0.146	0.007	89
V5	0.577	0.136	0.018	8	0.576	0.146	0.007	71
V6	0.555	0.145	0.02	10	0.559	0.148	0.007	72
V7	0.751	0.15	0.02	29	0.742	0.148	0.007	209
V8	0.876	0.132	0.018	68	0.877	0.129	0.006	514
V9	0.914	0.116	0.016	89	0.922	0.109	0.005	759
V10	0.963	0.071	0.01	140	0.959	0.077	0.004	1003

152   *Enterprise Risk Management*

From Table 6, it is evident that based on the simulated data the three worst performed vendors are V3, V4 and V5. This is consistent with that resulted from a Monte Carlo simulation to chance constrained programs in Section 3.1.

9.2.4 *Simulation and MOP*

We consider stochastic demand from various customers in simulation to MOP to see the change of vendor selection with respect to demand variation across various customers. As mentioned in Section 2.2, we can introduce weights to aggregate various objectives into a single criterion. Thus, the MOP binary programming problem can be solved using a series of linear programming models. To explain this, we develop the following algorithm to solve the MOP problem coupled with stochastic data and select two vendors for each customer.

Algorithm: Simulation in MOP

Step 1: Initialize the weights of different objectives, i.e., total purchase amount cost, items rejected rate and late delivery. Set the total number of candidate suppliers and total number of customer. Set upper and lower bounds for decision variables in Constraint (5) (6) (7) and (8).

Step 2: Define the distribution of cost, rejected rate, late delivery and demand, and set the value of related parameters. Set the number of simulation runs and generate experiment data according to defined distributions.

Step 3: denote by i the indicator of the candidate customer, set the initial value of i to unity.

Step 4: denote by j_1 the indicator of the 1st supplier and j_2 the indicator of the 2nd supplier; set the initial value of j_1 and j_2 to unity.

Step 5: if $j\_1 = j\_2$, set $j\_2 = j\_2 + 1$ and go to Step 6.

Step 6:   Solve the following linear program:

$$\min g_i(x_{i1}, x_{i2}) = \omega_1 \sum_{j=1}^{2} c_{ij} x_{ij} + \omega_2 \sum_{j=1}^{2} \beta_{ij} x_{ij} + \omega_3 \sum_{j=1}^{2} \lambda_{ij} x_{ij}$$

subject to :

$$x_{i1} + x_{i2} \geq D_i, \qquad \forall i$$

$$x_{ij} \leq u_{ij}^u, \qquad \forall i, j$$

$$x_{ij} \leq w_{ij}^u, \qquad \forall i, j$$

$$x_{ij} \geq u_{ij}^l, \qquad \forall i, j$$

$$x_{ij} \geq w_{ij}^l, \qquad \forall i, j$$

Denote by g_i^*, x_{i1}^* and x_{i2}^* the optimal objective value and optimal values of the variables to above linear program.

Step 7:   Set $j\_2 = j\_2 + 1$. If $j\_2 >$ the total number of candidate suppliers, set $j\_2 = 1$ and go to Step 8; Otherwise go to Step 5.

Step 8:   Set $j\_1 = j\_1 + 1$. If $j\_1 >$ the total number of candidate suppliers, set $j\_1 = 1$ and go to Step 9; Otherwise go to Step 5.

Step 9:   For the ith customer, find the combination (j_1, j_2), such that the objectives achieves minimum; Denote $J_i(j\_1, j\_2)$ the corresponding order quantity, i.e.,

$$J_i(j\_1, j\_2) = \arg\min_{j\_1, j\_2} f_i(x_{ij\_1}, x_{ij\_2})$$

Step 10:   Set $i = i + 1$. If $i >$ total number of customer, go to Step 11; Otherwise go to Step 4.

Step 11:   Generate statistic result after all simulation runs are done.

Using Matlab codes, the algorithm is implemented with the assumed distributions, calculating minimal cost, rejected items, and late items. We have carried out 600 simulation runs, which take around half an hour to run the codes.

Weight attached to three objectives are assumed to be independently identically distributed with uniform distribution in the interval $(0, 1)$. Figure 3 depicts simulated vendor data in 600 simulation runs and shows uncertainty in three criteria as simulation runs.

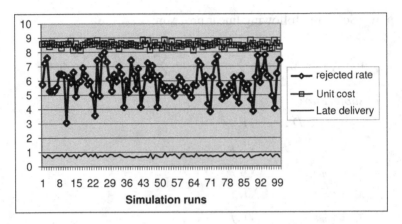

Figure 3: Simulated Vendor Data in 600 Simulation Runs

Table 7: Total Cost, Items Rejected and Late Rate for Each Customer

Customer (demand) number	Total cost: f_1^*		# items rejected f_1^*		# late items	
	Mean	Variance	Mean	Variance	Mean	Variance
D1	534.35	319.55	294.46	225.95	89.722	68.528
D2	500.53	298.82	276	211.55	84.055	64.118
D3	432.6	249.65	237.48	180.23	64.199	47.084
D4	412.89	245.86	214.34	163.65	54.135	42.89
D5	291.17	164.98	157.05	121.53	40.141	30.104
D6	264.68	156.44	138.26	105.99	32.43	27.271
D7	258.84	148.79	143.36	110.58	29.45	23.77
D8	262.18	147.26	148.19	119.47	27.107	22.42
D9	253.4	143.46	145.81	108.44	30.305	24.048
D10	245.37	138.31	153.32	117.11	25.064	19.753
D11	238.01	142.48	145.73	114.57	26.291	21.142
D12	242.26	146.42	140.6	114.97	24.323	18.821
D13	183.8	107.93	123.67	111.23	18.663	14.681
D14	166.65	98.947	110.33	93.515	14.47	10.876
D15	118.27	70.974	76.958	64.212	9.8612	7.6112
D16	70.697	42.862	46.37	37.778	6.0649	4.7379
D17	70.99	42.818	46.444	38.575	6.019	4.6311
D18	47.98	28.897	30.916	25.199	4.0655	3.1496
D19	48.288	28.962	31.021	23.696	4.0786	3.1405
D20	48.605	29.289	31.61	26.115	4.0817	3.0665

Table 8: Order Quantity from Two Suppliers

Quantity from the 1st vendor		Quantity from the 2nd vendor	
Mean	Variance	Mean	Variance
1520	499.6	1480	499.6
1416	399.68	1384	421.9
1080	97.98	1120	144.83
1000	0	1000	0
695	243.87	805	266.65
605	143.09	695	143.09
560	91.652	640	131.34
562	92.499	638	120.42
515	161.48	685	175.45
529	240.54	571	264.17
430	306.1	670	310.93
469	392.1	631	396.09
361.28	358.28	438.72	359.2
336.12	337.87	363.88	334.74
247.05	245.47	252.95	245.45
146.09	146.11	153.91	145.7
146.22	145.39	153.78	145.4
92.25	97.828	107.75	97.55
99.86	95.688	100.14	95.627
86.3	97.163	113.7	95.957

Table 7, 8 and 9 document the computation result. Table 7 presents the minimal total cost, items rejected and late rate for each customer. Table 8 presents optimal order quantity from two suppliers and Table 9 presents the probability of each customer's choice of suppliers.

From simulation results to MOP, we observe some interesting patterns: First, every vendor is likely to be selected by some buyers. Second, buyers expecting more demands are likely to have more total cost, items rejected and higher late delivery rate, which can be seen

Table 9: The Probability of Every Customer's Choice of Suppliers

	V1	V2	V3	V4	V5	V6	V7	V8	V9	V10
D1	0.13	0.15	0.16	0.08	0.11	0.05	0.16	0.33	0.42	0.41
D2	0.13	0.14	0.16	0.08	0.11	0.05	0.16	0.33	0.42	0.40
D3	0.13	0.16	0.18	0.10	0.12	0.06	0.2	0.36	0.49	0.18
D4	0.16	0.18	0.20	0.12	0.14	0.06	0.23	0.42	0.46	0.03
D5	0.14	0.18	0.19	0.11	0.13	0.07	0.21	0.38	0.35	0.20
D6	0.17	0.19	0.21	0.13	0.16	0.06	0.25	0.45	0.32	0.06
D7	0.20	0.24	0.24	0.08	0.14	0.08	0.29	0.33	0.26	0.09
D8	0.19	0.29	0.23	0.08	0.16	0.11	0.31	0.33	0.14	0.12
D9	0.19	0.24	0.23	0.05	0.15	0.09	0.32	0.31	0.15	0.23
D10	0.12	0.23	0.23	0.11	0.20	0.11	0.29	0.32	0.17	0.13
D11	0.14	0.22	0.20	0.14	0.17	0.10	0.27	0.28	0.17	0.24
D12	0.18	0.19	0.24	0.15	0.17	0.12	0.27	0.33	0.11	0.17
D13	0.14	0.21	0.16	0.19	0.15	0.26	0.26	0.23	0.15	0.18
D14	0.14	0.16	0.19	0.23	0.17	0.28	0.24	0.21	0.14	0.12
D15	0.14	0.15	0.18	0.25	0.19	0.33	0.25	0.20	0.12	0.12
D16	0.16	0.16	0.18	0.24	0.17	0.31	0.25	0.21	0.11	0.12
D17	0.18	0.17	0.20	0.25	0.18	0.31	0.22	0.23	0.11	0.13
D18	0.18	0.16	0.19	0.23	0.18	0.31	0.21	0.2	0.14	0.12
D19	0.19	0.17	0.19	0.23	0.19	0.31	0.21	0.19	0.13	0.12
D20	0.18	0.18	0.18	0.22	0.16	0.30	0.19	0.17	0.15	0.11

from Table 7. Third, from Table 9, when demand is high and demand uncertainty is severe, e.g., the demands faced by D1-6, the customers tend to select vendors V8, 9 and 10 in order to maintain low purchasing cost. It seems that these buyers cares more about cost than quality and on-time delivery since they are less likely to select V1-V4, which can provide better quality and on-time delivery. D15-20 are more likely to choose V4 and V6, which provide a mediate unit cost and reasonably good quality and on-time delivery. The probability of choosing V4, V5 and V6 by most buyers are low, which is consistent with the results from CCP, MOP and DEA simulation.

9.3 Conclusions

We have discussed three types of risk simulation models within supply chains: a Monte Carlo simulation to chance constrained programs, simulation to the multi-objective programming model and DEA simulation. Various risks in both supply and demand perspective are modeled in the form of probability and simulation of specific probability distribution in risk-embedded attributes is conducted. We have modeled a supply chain consisting of three levels and used simulated data with distributions empirically derived. We have proposed an algorithm to solve the proposed multi-objective programming model as well as the corresponding simulation model. Results from three models as well as simulation models are consistent with each other in selecting preferred suppliers taking risk factors into consideration. The results verified our proposed model and show that the proposed approach allows decision makers to perform trade-off analysis among expected costs, quality acceptance levels, and on-time delivery distributions. It also provides alternative tools to evaluate and improve supplier selection decisions in an uncertain SC environment.

Appendix A

Data Envelopment Analysis Basics

DEA is used to establish a best practice group amongst a set of observed units and to identify the units that are inefficient when compared to the best practice group. DEA also indicates the magnitude of the inefficiencies and improvements possible for the inefficient units. Consider n DMUs to be evaluated, DMU_j ($j = 1,2...n$) that consumes the amounts $X_j = \{x_{ij}\}$ of m different of inputs ($i = 1, 2, \ldots, m$) and produces the amounts $Y_j = \{y_{rj}\}$ of r outputs ($r = 1, \ldots, s$). The input oriented efficiency of a particular DMU_0 under the assumption of constant returns to scale can be obtained from the following primal-dual linear programs (input-oriented CCR model).

$$\min_{\theta,\lambda,s^+,s^-} \quad z_0 = \theta - \varepsilon \cdot \vec{1} s^+ - \varepsilon \cdot \vec{1} s^-$$

$$s.t. \qquad Y\lambda - s^+ = Y_0 \tag{1}$$
$$\theta X_0 - X\lambda - s^- = 0$$
$$\lambda, \; s^+, s^- \geq 0$$

Where s^+ and s^- are the slacks in the system.

$$\max_{\mu,\nu} \quad w_0 = \mu^T Y_0$$

$$s.t. \qquad \nu^T X_0 = 1$$
$$\mu^T Y - \nu^T X \leq 0 \tag{2}$$
$$-\mu^T \leq -\varepsilon \cdot \vec{1}$$
$$-\nu^T \leq -\varepsilon \cdot \vec{1}$$

Performing a DEA analysis requires the solution of n linear programming problems of the above form, one for each DMU. The optimal value of the variable θ indicates the proportional reduction of all inputs for DMU_0 that will move it onto the frontier which is the envelopment surface defined by the efficient DMUs in the sample. A DMU is termed efficient if and only if the optimal value $\theta*$ is equal to 1 and all the slack variables are zero.

Endnotes

1. Sahin, F., Robinson, E.P. (2002). Flow coordination and information sharing in supply chains: Review, implications, and directions for future research. *Decision Sciences* 33:4, 505-536.
2. Choi, T.Y., Dooley, K.J., Rungtusanatham, M. (2001). Supply networks and complex adaptive systems: Control versus emergence. *Journal of Operations Management* 19, 351-366.
3. Xu, K., Dong, Y. (2004). Information gaming in demand collaboration and supply chain performance, *Journal of Business Logistics* 25:1, 121-144.

4. Callioni, G., de Montros, X., Slagmulder, R., Van Wassenhove, L.N., Wright, L. (2005). Inventory-driven costs. *Harvard Business Review* 82:3, 135-140.

5. Kremic, T., Tukel, O.I., Rom, W.O. (2006), Outsourcing decision support: A survey of benefits, risks, and decision factors. *Supply Chain Management: An International Journal* 11:6, 467-482.

6. Cohen, M.A., Lee, H.L. (1988). Strategic analysis of integrated production–distribution systems: Models and methods. Operations Research 36:2, 216–228.; Lee, H.L., Billington, C. (1993). Material management in decentralized supply chain. Operations Research 41:5, 835–847; Thomas, D.J., Griffin, P.M. (1996). Coordinated supply chain management. European Journal of Operational Research 94:1, 1–15; Graves, S.C., Willems, S.P. (2000). Optimizing strategic safety stock placement in supply chains. Manufacturing & Service Operations Management 2:1, 68–83; Goetschalckx, M., Vidal, C.J., Dogan, K. (2002). Modeling and design of global logistics systems: A review of integrated strategic and tactical models and design algorithms. European Journal of Operational Research 143:1, 1–18; Chen, I.J., Paulraj, A. (2004). Understanding supply chain management: Critical research and a theoretical framework. International Journal of Production Research 42:1, 131–163.

7. Narasimhan, R., Talluri, S., Mahapatra, S.K. (2006). Multiproduct, multicriteria model for supplier selection with product life-cycle considerations. *Decision Sciences* 37:4, 577-603.

8. Ojala, M., Hallikas, J. (2006). Investment decision-making in supplier networks: Management of risk. *International Journal of Production Economics* 104, 201-213.

9. Li, Q. (2007). Risk, risk aversion and the optimal time to produce. *IIE Transactions* 39, 145-158.

10. Barbarosoğlu, G., Yazgaç, T. (2000). A decision support model for customer value assessment and supply quota allocation. *Production Planning & Control* 11:6, 608-616.

11. Rabelo, L., Eskandari, H., Shaalan, T., Helal, M. (2007). Value chain analysis using hybrid simulation and AHP. *International Journal*

of Production Economics 105, 536-547; Kirkwood, C.W., Slaven, M.P., Maltz, A. (2005). Improving supply-chain-reconfiguration decisions at IBM. *Interfaces* 35:6, 460-473.

12. Wang, J., Shu, Y.-F. (2007). A possibilistic decision model for new product supply chain design. *European Journal of Operational Research* 177, 1044-1061.

13. Gaur, S., Ravindran, A.R. (2006). A bi-criteria model for the inventory aggregation problem under risk pooling. *Computers & Industrial Engineering* 51, 482-501.

14. Talluri, S., Narasimhan, R., Nair, A. (2006), Vendor performance with supply risk: A chance-constrained DEA approach. *International Journal of Production Economics* 100, 212-222.

15. Wu, D., Olson, D.L. (2007). A comparison of stochastic dominance and stochastic DEA for vendor evaluation. *International Journal of Production Research* to be published.

16. Barbarosoğlu, G. (2000). An integrated supplier-buyer model for improving supply chain coordination. *Production Planning & Control* 11:8, 732-741; Talluri, S., Narasimhan, R., Nair, A. (2006), Vendor performance with supply risk: A chance-constrained DEA approach. *International Journal of Production Economics* 100, 212-222.

17. Narasimhan et al. (2006), op cit.

18. Steuer, R.E. (1986). *Multiple Criteria Optimization: Theory, Computation, and Application.* New York: John Wiley & Sons.

19. Narasimhan et al. (2006), op cit.

20. Narasimhan et al. (2006), op cit.

21. Evans, J.R., Olson, D.L. (2002). *Introduction to Simulation and Risk Analysis 2nd ed.*. Upper Saddle River, NJ: Prentice Hall.

Chapter 10

Credit Risk Analysis

> Describes measures often used to gauge financial risk
> Reviews the use of credit scoring to assess risk
> Demonstrates methods on real credit scoring data

This chapter discusses how different risk measures in ERM can act to integrate operations and finance functions. We will demonstrate risk measures in a credit scoring operational decision for a financial services firm.

To build/review a behavioral scoring model, we propose two categories of risk measures: risk performance measures and risk monitoring measures. Performance validation focuses in credit rating on two key aspects: discriminatory power (risk discrimination) and predictive accuracy (model calibration). Discriminatory power generally focuses on the model's ability to rank-order risk, while predictive accuracy focuses on the model's ability to predict outcomes accurately (e.g. probability of defaults, loss given defaults, etc.). Various statistical measures can be used to test the discriminatory power and predictive accuracy of a model.[1] Commonly used measures in credit rating include the lift/CAP curve, divergence, and the Kolmogorov-Smirnov (KS) statistic. Monitoring measures aim to diagnose the causality of the problem diagnosed by the performance risk measures. Two risk monitoring measures are used: population stability index and characteristic analysis.

10.1 Financial Risk Measures

The **cumulative accuracy profile (CAP)** curve, also known as "power curve" or "lift", visually demonstrates the rank-ordering ability of a model over its entire range of risk scores for a particular time horizon. For example, the dot curved line in Figure 1 shows the performance of the model being evaluated. The point (x, y) indicates that the bottom x% of the population with lowest (riskiest) scores captures y% of the defaulted companies. The thick straight line depicts a perfect model that captures 100% of defaults within a fraction of the population equal to the default rate of the sample.   The 45-degree dash line represents the random model. The closer the dark curved line is to the perfect model, the better the model performs.

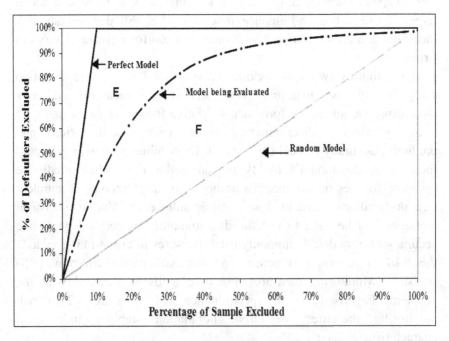

Figure 1: Example of a CAP Curve and Accuracy Ratio

Divergence measures the ability of a scoring system to separate good accounts from bad accounts. This statistic is the squared difference between the mean score of the Good and Bad' accounts divided by their average variance:

$$(\mu_g - \mu_b)^2 / ((V_g + V_b)/2) ,$$

where μ_g, μ_b represent the mean of the good and bad population and V_g, V_b represent the variance of the good and bad population respectively. The higher the divergence, the larger the separation of scores between Good and Bad accounts (see Figure 2). Ideally, 'good' accounts should be highly concentrated in the high score ranges and conversely, 'bad' accounts should be highly concentrated in the low score ranges.

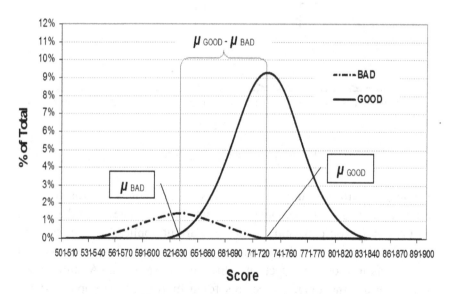

Figure 2: Illustration of Divergence

Kolmogorov-Smirnov (K-S) Test: Ideally, the Bad curve should increase more quickly at the low score ranges, where these accounts should be found if the model is accurately rank ordering. Conversely, a low percentage of Good accounts should be found in the low score range and then show a higher concentration in the high score range (see Figure 3). The K-S Statistic identifies the maximum separation (percentage) between the cumulative percentage of Goods vs. Bads at any given score. It may also be used to provide a cut-off score to assess applicants. The K-S statistic ranges from 0 to 100%.

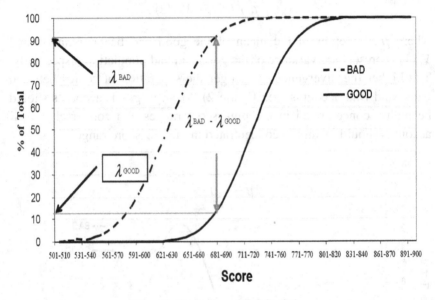

Figure 3: Illustration of K-S Statistics

Population stability index (PSI): This index gauges the discrepancy between the original development population used to generate the model and the population consisting of all the current applicants. It is used to measure comparatively the distribution of the scores between the two populations in order to detect any shifts in the samples. Assume p_i, q_i, $i = 1,...,m$ are the ranges of scores for a more recent sample and for chosen benchmark, respectively. The PSI is calculated as follows:

$$PSI = \sum_{i=1}^{m}(p_i - q_i)*\ln(p_i/q_i)/100$$

The following indices may be used as guidelines: an index of 0.10 or less is indicative of no real change between the samples; a score between

0.10 and 0.25 indicates some shift; and an index greater 0.25 signifies a definite change that should be further analyzed.

Characteristic analysis: For each characteristic the change in the contribution of that characteristic to the overall score is calculated based on the change in the distribution of the characteristic over two different observation windows. Assume a characteristic has attributes $1,\ldots,k$ with associated points $p_i, i = 1,\ldots,k$. If the distribution of that characteristic in the first (development) and second (current) observation window is described by the percentages $q_i, s_i, i = 1,\ldots,k$, respectively, that satisfy

$$\sum_{i=1}^{k} q_i = 100 \quad \text{and} \quad \sum_{i=1}^{k} s_i = 100 .$$

The change p in the overall score due to the change in the characteristic distribution among the k attributes is calculated based on the formula

$$p = \sum_{i=1}^{k} p_i * (s_i - q_i) .$$

The higher the change p, the higher the impact of that characteristic on the overall model score.

Similarly, one can calculate a chi-square statistic as follows:

$$chi - sq = \sum_{i=1}^{k} (s_i - q_i)^2 / q_i .$$

Larger the values, more significant the change in the distribution of characteristic's attributes since model development.

10.2 Credit Scoring

Credit and behavioural scoring are very important finance operations. According to the annual reports of the credit bureau, an adult in the UK or US is scored on average at least once a week.[2] There are two main types of retail scoring models: Adjudication Models and Behaviour

Models. The Adjudication Model is a credit scoring model used for assessing risk at the point of application, e.g., approval decisions for new customers, loan amounts, limit setting. The Behaviour Model is a credit scoring model used for assessing risk of existing customers for "actioning" purposes, e.g., limits increases, renewals, collection strategies. We discuss various modeling operational decisions and validate in the section the Early Collections Behaviour Model that is currently being used in a big bank. The bank experienced three stages of operational decisions in employing credit modeling tools. The first stage is prior to 2003,[3] when the bank outsourced its decision tool to an external vendor. This tool predicted the likelihood of an account with 60-120 days delinquency curing within the subsequent 3 months. The scorecard used the real-time bureau report from the vendor, and it is scored on a daily basis. After a model validation in December 2001 with the conclusion that the outsourced decision tool was underperforming, a second operational decision was made that a new model should be developed internally that outperforms the existing tool. This new scorecard was supposed to utilize the quarterly bureau data which will reduce the bureau cost for Early Stage Collection. The model was developed in 2003, separately for two subpopulations: Portfolio1 and Portfolio2, to be used in the early stage collections strategies. The third operational decision problem occurs simply because that we feel the model is aging and possible updating is needed.

10.2.1 *Modeling*

The Early Collections models was developed predict the likelihood that a personal account being in collections will cure within the subsequent 60 days (by itself or due to collections effort). The portfolios included in the modeling are Unsecured Personal Line of Credit, Unsecured and Secured Personal Loan, and Demand Deposit (Checking and Savings). The Early Collections Scorecard was developed based on 6 months shifting observation period starting September 1, 2001 and ending May 1, 2002. The performance window was 2 months. Prior to the variable creation, various account and portfolio exclusions are considered. For example, Small business, commercial, and corporate portfolios, Duplicate records from false cure accounts, or Duplicate records due to loan branch conversions are excluded. An account is defined "bad" if, based on the Delinquency Management (DM) rules, does not cure within 60 days since entry into the DM system or if it is written-off. Any other account is considered "good".

The methodology used is Logistic Regression and the outcome is a probability to become bad (expressed in percentages). Logistic Regression models are developed for each of the following two subpopulations: Portfolio1 and Portfolio2. The former is comprised of Checking and Savings accounts customers with or without an authorized Overdraft Protection (ODP) service and occupies one third of the portfolio, while the latter is comprised of Unsecured Lines of Credit, Secured and Unsecured personal loans customers and occupies two thirds of the portfolio.

A predictive model is created by analyzing past behaviors/ characteristics of a customer to predict the future behavior using statistical techniques. The time period in which historical data obtained and used to build the model is defined as Observation Window. The Outcome Window is the time period in which the actual account performance data is observed to pinpoint the event.

To develop the model, shifting observation and performance windows is used. The observation windows for model development are defined as September 1, 2001 to February 28, 2002, October 1, 2001 to March 31, 2002 and November 1, 2001 to April 30, 2002. The characteristics of customers and accounts in collections will be analyzed as of March 1, 2002, April 1, 2002 and May 1, 2002, to determine what information will separate accounts that will perform in a certain way in the outcome window from accounts that will perform differently. For this model, the performance data from March 1, 2002 to April 30, 2002, April 1, 2002 to May 31, 2002 and May 1, 2002 to June 30, 2002 will be used.

10.3 Data

Table 1 illustrates the bad rate for each product segment. We report in the table the frequency and percentage of both Portfolio1 and Portfolio2.

Enterprise Risk Management

Table 1: Bad Rate by Product Segment for Portfolio1 and Portfolio2

		Portfolio1			
		CASUAL ODP	ODP	ODP NO DEP	Total
Good	Frequency	56343	19140	11596	87079
	Percent	41.61	14.14	8.56	64.31
Bad	Frequency	37996	7881	2447	48324
	Percent	28.06	5.82	1.81	35.69
Total	Frequency	94339	27021	14043	135403
	Percent	69.67	19.96	10.37	100.00
		Portfolio2			
		LON	SELECT LI NE	STUD LIN E	Total
Good	Frequency	52217	191899	15582	259698
	Percent	18.93	69.59	5.65	94.17
Bad	Frequency	6201	9222	651	16074
	Percent	2.25	3.34	0.24	5.83
Total	Frequency	58418	201121	16233	275772
	Percent	21.18	72.93	5.89	100.00

As for the product segments, the bad rate for Portfolio1 was 35.69% while the bad rate for Portfolio2 was 5.83%. Portfolio1 consists of the following products: ODP, Casual ODP and ODP with no deposit. Portfolio2 is compromised of the following products: Loan, Unsecured LOC and Student LOC.

There are 411,175 records in the out of time period: January – March 2005. The overall bad rate for the population is 15.66%, whereas the development population bad rate was 10.8%.

Table 2 presents the set of P1 (Labeled with D) and P2 (Labeled with V) predictors, with most able to predict the bad outcome being DM system history, as well as some customer level data elements.

For the purposes of the model validation, accounts that entered DM System during the months of January, February and March of 2005 were used for the analysis. The Observation Window includes 6 months and the Performance Window includes 2 months. Table 3 presents the statistic values overall and by product. Table 3 indicates that the structure

Table 2: Variables and Sources

Label	Portfolio2 Predictor	Source
V1	Average 30 days delinquent amount in last 6 months	Account level
V2	Average Over limit Amount in Last 6 Months	Account level
V3	Account Delinquent Suspend Indicator	Account level
V4	Number of accounts in Collections in last 6 months	DM activity log
V5	Number of accounts in DM in last 6 months	DM activity log
V6	Months Since Oldest R / O type	Credit Bureau
V7	Past Due Trades	Credit Bureau
V8	R Trades Utilization Rate in last 12 months	Credit Bureau
V9	Trades Ever 90 or derogatory public record	Credit Bureau
V10	Initial LOC limit	Account level
V11	# Account in collections among join customers	Customer level
V12	Customer Tenure in Months	Customer level
V13	Total Number of Accounts	Customer level
Label	Portfolio1 Predictor	Source
D1	Average Demand Deposit Balance in last 6 months	Account level
D2	Demand Deposit Balance in the latest month end	Account level
D3	Average days in DM in last 6 months	DM Account level
D4	Average total payment	Credit Bureau
D5	Months since the oldest trade	Credit Bureau
D6	Total Past Sure Trades	Credit Bureau
D7	Average Customer Age	Customer level
D8	Total Number of Accounts	Customer level

of the portfolio has changed since development: the Portfolio1 decreased by 61%, while the Portfolio2 increased by 26%. As well, the Portfolio1 bad rate increased by 67%, while the Portfolio2 bad rate decreased by 9%.

Table 3: Variables and Sources

Sample	Entered in DM	# Accounts	Bad Rate
Development	9/1/2001 – 11/30/2001	294,423	10.8%
Out-of-Time (OOT) Validation	1/1/2005 – 3/30/2005	411,175	15.7%
Sample	Portfolio1 / Portfolio2 Split	Bad Rate Portfolio1	Bad Rate Portfolio2
Development	30%/70%	21.4%	6.4%
Out-of-Time (OOT) Validation	11.8%/88.2%	35.7%	5.83%

10.4 Results

The models were implemented in SAS Enterprise Miner, generating logistic regression models for Portfolio1 and Portfolio2. Denote by p a probability to of becoming bad, the final behavioral scoring models used in the scorecards are:

Portfolio1 Model Formula:

$$\text{Log}\left(\frac{p}{1-p}\right) = -1.326639807 - 0.004492646 * D1 - 0.007030679 * D2 -$$
$0.009343651*D3 + 0.0035701241*D4 - 0.003331156*D5 -$
$0.006894189*D6 - 0.00302576*D7 - 0.00725949*D8$

Portfolio2 Model Formula:

$$\text{Log}\left(\frac{p}{1-p}\right) = -2.67154569122668 - 0.00488430318206 * V1 -$$
$0.00788618949426*V2 - 0.00286984353371*V3 - 0.00812143636106*V4 -$
$0.00210241886193*V5 - 0.005112410222242*V6 - 0.00375079491432*V7 -$
$0.00392262457473*V8 - 0.00390775062737*V9 -$
$0.00489255281705*V10 - 0.00432268961044*V11 -$
$0.00444270446698*V12 - 0.00733305326916*V13$

In order to validate the relative effectiveness of the behavior model, we conduct statistic analysis and report results for the following statistical measures: Divergence Test, Kolmogorov-Smirnov (K-S) Test, Lorenz Curve, and population stability index. We also conduct characteristics analysis for Portfolio1 and Portfolio2 results, respectively. We present statistical results and discussion for three populations: Portfolio1 (P1), Portfolio2 (P2), and Overall Population including both.

10.4.1 *Results from overall population*

Table 4 documents diagnostic statistics for the three samples from Overall Population.

Overall, as can be seen from the KS and divergence values in Table 2, the models continue to rank-order well (KS = 44.4). Anyway, the Divergence value has decreased to 0.81 from a value of 1.1 when comparing against developed data. An increase in the mean Good score or a decrease in the mean Bad score for the 2005 data indicates that the model is not separating the good and bad accounts as effectively relative to the 2002 data. This indicates that the two curves are converging.

The population stability index can be used to estimate the change between the samples, which provides insight into whether or not the behavior model is being used to score a different population. Table 5 presents a detailed score distribution report from Overall Portfolio.

Table 4: Overall Portfolio Performance

Overall Population	Model	# Goods	Mean Goods	St dev Goods	# Bads	Mean Bads	St dev Bads
Development, 2002	All	262801	88.6	94.0	31622	212.6	137.7
Out of Time, 2002	All	202993	85.1	82.8	27910	206.5	117.4
Validation, 2005	All	346777	120.3	95.8	64398	208.0	99.3

Overall Population	Divergence	K-S Statistic	K-S Score
Development, 2002	1.1	46.6	99
Out of Time, 2002	1.43	52.2	117
Validation, 2005	0.81	44.4	132

Enterprise Risk Management

Table 5: Population Stability Distribution from Overall Portfolio

Final Score Interval	Development Pop.	Current Pop.	% Share of Dev. Pop.	% Share of Current Pop.	A5-A4	A5/A4
A1	A2	A3	A4	A5	A6	A7
641+	619	341	0.21%	0.08%	-0.001	0.396
621-640	198	150	0.07%	0.04%	0.000	0.545
601-620	192	159	0.06%	0.04%	0.000	0.596
581-600	213	216	0.07%	0.05%	0.000	0.730
561-580	309	387	0.10%	0.09%	0.000	0.901
541-560	296	524	0.10%	0.13%	0.000	1.274
521-540	390	504	0.13%	0.12%	0.000	0.930
501-520	436	842	0.15%	0.20%	0.001	1.390
481-500	475	770	0.16%	0.19%	0.000	1.166
461-480	567	942	0.19%	0.23%	0.000	1.195
441-460	552	1092	0.19%	0.27%	0.001	1.423
421-440	717	1440	0.24%	0.35%	0.001	1.445
401-420	772	1633	0.26%	0.40%	0.001	1.522
381-400	1121	1858	0.38%	0.45%	0.001	1.193
361-380	1681	2692	0.57%	0.65%	0.001	1.152
341-360	1897	3291	0.64%	0.80%	0.002	1.248
321-340	2273	3900	0.77%	0.95%	0.002	1.235
301-320	2681	4217	0.91%	1.03%	0.001	1.132
281-300	3166	5570	1.07%	1.35%	0.003	1.266
261-280	6272	11924	2.12%	2.90%	0.008	1.368
241-260	7881	14501	2.66%	3.53%	0.009	1.324
221-240	9404	19570	3.18%	4.76%	0.016	1.497
201-220	10286	23338	3.48%	5.68%	0.022	1.633
181-200	9955	20276	3.36%	4.93%	0.016	1.466
161-180	10454	24179	3.53%	5.88%	0.023	1.664
141-160	9944	19743	3.36%	4.80%	0.014	1.429
121-140	10606	22465	3.58%	5.46%	0.019	1.524
101-120	12023	25939	4.06%	6.31%	0.022	1.552
81-100	15778	32009	5.33%	7.78%	0.025	1.460
61-80	22132	44647	7.48%	10.86%	0.034	1.452
41-60	34339	55788	11.61%	13.57%	0.020	1.169
21-40	59128	53269	19.99%	12.96%	-0.070	0.648
0-20	59102	12999	19.98%	3.16%	-0.168	0.158

Table 5: Population Stability Distribution from Overall Portfolio part 2

Final Score Interval	LN(A7)	Contribution to Index [A8*A6]	Ascending Cum %.A5	Ascending Cum %.A4
A1	A8	A9	A10	A11
641+	-0.925	0.001	0.08%	0.21%
621-640	-0.607	0.000	0.12%	0.28%
601-620	-0.518	0.000	0.16%	0.34%
581-600	-0.315	0.000	0.21%	0.41%
561-580	-0.104	0.000	0.30%	0.52%
541-560	0.242	0.000	0.43%	0.62%
521-540	-0.073	0.000	0.55%	0.75%
501-520	0.329	0.000	0.76%	0.90%
481-500	0.154	0.000	0.95%	1.06%
461-480	0.179	0.000	1.18%	1.25%
441-460	0.353	0.000	1.44%	1.44%
421-440	0.368	0.000	1.79%	1.68%
401-420	0.420	0.001	2.19%	1.94%
381-400	0.176	0.000	2.64%	2.32%
361-380	0.142	0.000	3.30%	2.89%
341-360	0.222	0.000	4.10%	3.53%
321-340	0.211	0.000	5.04%	4.30%
301-320	0.124	0.000	6.07%	5.20%
281-300	0.236	0.001	7.42%	6.27%
261-280	0.313	0.002	10.32%	8.39%
241-260	0.281	0.002	13.85%	11.06%
221-240	0.404	0.006	18.61%	14.23%
201-220	0.490	0.011	24.29%	17.71%
181-200	0.382	0.006	29.22%	21.08%
161-180	0.509	0.012	35.10%	24.61%
141-160	0.357	0.005	39.90%	27.97%
121-140	0.421	0.008	45.36%	31.55%
101-120	0.440	0.010	51.67%	35.62%
81-100	0.378	0.009	59.46%	40.95%
61-80	0.373	0.013	70.32%	48.43%
41-60	0.156	0.003	83.88%	60.04%
21-40	-0.433	0.030	96.84%	80.02%
0-20	-1.844	0.310	100.00%	100.00%

Note: Population Stability Index (sum of contribution): 0.433
The contribution to index can be interpreted as follows:
PSI ≤ 0.10 Indicates little to no difference between the development
score distribution and the current score distribution.
0.10 ≤ PSI ≤ 0.25 Indicates some change has taken place.
0.25 ≤ PSI Indicates a shift in the score distribution has occurred.

As mentioned in Section 4, a stability index of < 0.10 indicates an insignificant shift, 0.10-0.25 requires some investigation and > 0.25 means that a major change has taken place between the populations being compared. Overall, the distribution has shifted as indicated by the Stability Index value of 0.433.   However, the majority of the shift has occurred in the 0-20 points category.

10.4.2 *Results from portfolio 1*

Table 6 presents diagnostic statistics for the three samples from Portfolio1. The corresponding lift curve is depicted in Figures 5. In a data set that has been sorted by the scores in ascending order (if a low score corresponds to a risky account), the perfect model would capture all the 'bads' as quickly as possible. The lift curve assesses a model's ability to effectively rank order these accounts. For example, if 15% of the accounts were bad, the ideal or exact model would capture all these bads within the 15th percentile of the Score Distribution (the x-axis). Similarly, the KS and Divergence statistics determine how well the models distinguished between 'good' and 'bad' accounts by assessing the properties of their respective distributions.

Table 6: Portfolio 1 Performance

Population	# Goods	Mean Goods	St dev Goods	# Bads	Mean Bads	St dev Bads
Development, 2002	67250	179.866	99.959	18246	253	117
Out of Time, 2002	37526	191.914	99.923	16043	251	98
Validation, 2005	87079	202.15	103.983	48324	225	92

Population	Divergence	K-S Statistic	K-S Score
Development, 2002	0.451	26.37	196
Out of Time, 2002	0.367	26.67	199
Validation, 2005	0.054	13.78	172

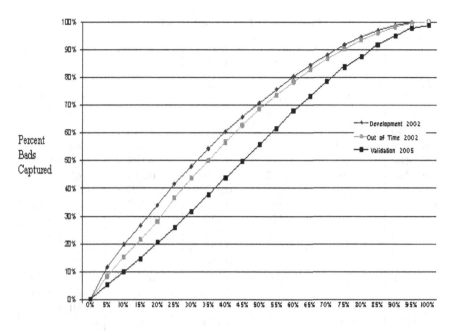

Figure 5: Lift Curve of Portfolio1 Performance Sample

The summary statistics above show deterioration in the Divergence and K-S statistics for the validation 2005 data. Notice that both the mean Good score and the variation associated with the good accounts have increased. The validation results indicate that the performance of the Portfolio1 model has deteriorated over time. The maximum difference in lift between the two datasets is 16.67%, occurring at 40% into the distribution.

Table 7 presents a detailed score distribution report from Portfolio1. As illustrated in the table, the score distribution is still stable since development. The population stability index is .056, indicating that little or no difference between the 2005 validation data and the development data exists.

Enterprise Risk Management

Table 7: Population Stability Distribution from Portfolio1

Final Score Interval	Development Pop.	Current Pop.	% Share of Dev. Pop.	% Share of Current Pop.	A5-A4	A5/A4
A1	A2	A3	A4	A5	A6	A7
641+	336	225	0.39%	0.17%	-0.002	0.423
621-640	124	114	0.15%	0.08%	-0.001	0.580
601-620	115	96	0.13%	0.07%	-0.001	0.527
581-600	141	149	0.16%	0.11%	-0.001	0.667
561-580	203	312	0.24%	0.23%	0.000	0.970
541-560	180	427	0.21%	0.32%	0.001	1.498
521-540	237	383	0.28%	0.28%	0.000	1.020
501-520	280	621	0.33%	0.46%	0.001	1.400
481-500	274	562	0.32%	0.42%	0.001	1.295
461-480	336	649	0.39%	0.48%	0.001	1.220
441-460	314	729	0.37%	0.54%	0.002	1.466
421-440	412	1002	0.48%	0.74%	0.003	1.536
401-420	412	1086	0.48%	0.80%	0.003	1.664
381-400	702	1229	0.82%	0.91%	0.001	1.105
361-380	1215	1836	1.42%	1.36%	-0.001	0.954
341-360	1329	2305	1.55%	1.70%	0.001	1.095
321-340	1675	2777	1.96%	2.05%	0.001	1.047
301-320	1913	2891	2.24%	2.14%	-0.001	0.954
281-300	2299	3780	2.69%	2.79%	0.001	1.038
261-280	5160	9712	6.04%	7.17%	0.011	1.188
241-260	6513	11728	7.62%	8.66%	0.010	1.137
221-240	7607	15830	8.90%	11.69%	0.028	1.314
201-220	8184	15313	9.57%	11.31%	0.017	1.181
181-200	7412	13777	8.67%	10.17%	0.015	1.174
161-180	7027	10489	8.22%	7.75%	-0.005	0.943
141-160	6015	8406	7.04%	6.21%	-0.008	0.882
121-140	5290	6511	6.19%	4.81%	-0.014	0.777
101-120	4458	5248	5.21%	3.88%	-0.013	0.743
81-100	3685	4257	4.31%	3.14%	-0.012	0.729
61-80	2820	3892	3.30%	2.87%	-0.004	0.871
41-60	2867	3597	3.35%	2.66%	-0.007	0.792
21-40	2538	2731	2.97%	2.02%	-0.010	0.679
0-20	3423	2739	4.00%	2.02%	-0.020	0.505

Table 7: Population Stability Distribution from Portfolio1 part 2

Final Score Interval	LN(A7)	Contribution to Index [A8*A6]	Ascending Cum %.A5	Ascending Cum %.A4
A1	A8	A9	A10	A11
641+	-0.861	0.002	0.17%	0.39%
621-640	-0.544	0.000	0.25%	0.54%
601-620	-0.640	0.000	0.32%	0.67%
581-600	-0.405	0.000	0.43%	0.84%
561-580	-0.030	0.000	0.66%	1.07%
541-560	0.404	0.000	0.98%	1.29%
521-540	0.020	0.000	1.26%	1.56%
501-520	0.337	0.000	1.72%	1.89%
481-500	0.259	0.000	2.13%	2.21%
461-480	0.199	0.000	2.61%	2.60%
441-460	0.382	0.001	3.15%	2.97%
421-440	0.429	0.001	3.89%	3.45%
401-420	0.509	0.002	4.69%	3.93%
381-400	0.100	0.000	5.60%	4.76%
361-380	-0.047	0.000	6.96%	6.18%
341-360	0.091	0.000	8.66%	7.73%
321-340	0.046	0.000	10.71%	9.69%
301-320	-0.047	0.000	12.85%	11.93%
281-300	0.037	0.000	15.64%	14.62%
261-280	0.173	0.002	22.81%	20.65%
241-260	0.128	0.001	31.47%	28.27%
221-240	0.273	0.008	43.16%	37.17%
201-220	0.167	0.003	54.47%	46.74%
181-200	0.160	0.002	64.65%	55.41%
161-180	-0.059	0.000	72.39%	63.63%
141-160	-0.125	0.001	78.60%	70.66%
121-140	-0.252	0.003	83.41%	76.85%
101-120	-0.297	0.004	87.29%	82.07%
81-100	-0.315	0.004	90.43%	86.38%
61-80	-0.138	0.001	93.30%	89.67%
41-60	-0.233	0.002	95.96%	93.03%
21-40	-0.386	0.004	97.98%	96.00%
0-20	-0.683	0.014	100.00%	100.00%

Note: Population Stability Index (sum of contribution): 0.056

Enterprise Risk Management

Table 8: Characteristics Analysis

Variable	# Attribute	Chi-sqr Stats	Variable	# Attribute	Chi-sqr Stats
V1	6	3.57	D1	7	10.63
V2	4	5.81	D2	4	.57
V3	2	1.37	D3	7	5.41
V4	3	377.06	D4	5	11.66
V5	2	.11	D5	6	8.56
V6	5	.98	D6	6	2.23
V7	8	1.9	D7	7	10.01
V8	6	.53	D8	8	10.09
V9	4	1.27			
V10	5	6.34			
V11	3	10.25			
V12	7	3.16			
V13	5	2.59			

We now conduct characteristics analysis for Portfolio1 model. The results are presented in Table 8. Table 9 demonstrates the characteristics analysis details for two characteristics: Total Number of Accounts and Average Customer Age. The Characteristic Analysis reveals that statistically significant changes in the characteristics have occurred since the development for several attributes. The Chi-Square Goodness of Fit test uses sample data to test hypotheses about the shape or proportions of a population distribution. The test determines how well the observed sample proportions fit the expected population proportions. Table 8 indicates that large changes are attributed to the following variables: Average Total Payment, Average Demand Deposit Balance in Last 6 Months, Total Number of Accounts, Average Customer Age, and Months Since Oldest CB Trade.

It appears that the majority of the changes are occurring where the account holder has little history with the bank. For example, from Table 9, the average customer age less or equal to 22 has increased to 19% from 10% in the development sample. As well, the majority of our accounts in collections have only 1 account with the bank, which is as expected, however this has increased by 13% from the development phase.

Table 9: Characteristics Analysis Demonstration

	Attribute	Devel. Population Frequency		Out of Time Pop. Frequency		Change
Total Number of Accounts	1	24453	28.7%	55849	41.2%	12.6%
	2	20159	23.6%	33283	24.6%	0.9%
	3	13897	16.3%	18233	13.5%	-2.8%
	4	8175	9.6%	9968	7.4%	-2.2%
	5	5345	6.3%	6111	4.5%	-1.8%
	6-7	6371	7.5%	6680	4.9%	-2.5%
	8-10	4168	4.9%	3524	2.6%	-2.3%
	11+	2704	3.2%	1755	1.3%	-1.9%
	Totals	85272	100%	135403	100%	/
Average Cust. Age	<=22	8833	10.4%	26019	19.2%	8.9%
	23-26	8667	10.2%	15129	11.2%	1.0%
	27-35	18848	22.1%	30067	22.2%	0.1%
	36-43	19124	22.4%	26883	19.9%	-2.6%
	44-51	14736	17.3%	20676	15.3%	-2.0%
	52-58	8321	9.8%	10341	7.6%	-2.1%
	59+	6743	7.9%	6288	4.6%	-3.3%
	Totals	85272	100.0%	135403	100.0%	/

10.4.3 *Results from portfolio 2*

Table 10 documents diagnostic statistics for the 3 samples from Portfolio1. The corresponding lift curve is depicted in Figures 6.

Table 10: Portfolio 2 Performance

Population	# Goods	Mean Goods	St dev Goods	# Bads	Mean Bads	St dev Bads
Development, 2002	196750	58	68	13613	159	145
Out of Time, 2002	165467	61	56	11867	147	115
Validation, 2005	259698	93	75	16074	157	102

Population	Divergence	K-S Statistic	K-S Score
Development, 2002	0.790	42.63	66
Out of Time, 2002	0.902	42.77	75
Validation, 2005	0.508	34.39	94

The summary statistics in Table 10 show some deterioration in the Divergence and K-S statistics for the validation 2005 data. Notice that both the mean Good score and the variation associated with the good accounts have increased.

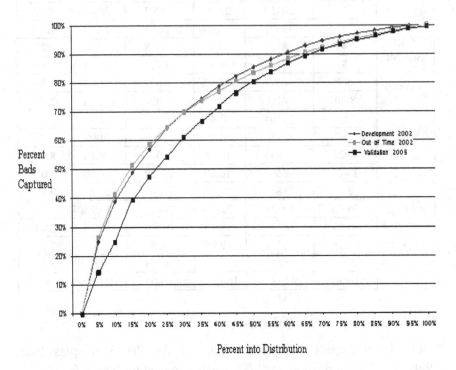

Figure 6: Lift Curve of Portfolio2 Performance Sample

The validation results indicate that the performance of the Portfolio2 model has deteriorated somewhat over time. The maximum difference in lift of Figure 6 between the two datasets is 16%, occurring at the 10th percentile into the distribution.

Table 11 presents a detailed score distribution report from Portfolio2. In terms of the population stability, the score distribution is not stable relative to the development data. The population stability index is .687, indicating that a shift in the score distribution has occurred. Again, the majority of the shift has occurred in the 0-20 score range.

Table 11: Population Stability Distribution from Portfolio2

Final Score Interval	Development Pop.	Current Pop.	% Share of Dev. Pop.	% Share of Current Pop.	A5-A4	A5/A4
A1	A2	A3	A4	A5	A6	A7
641+	283	116	0.13%	0.04%	-0.001	0.313
621-640	74	36	0.04%	0.01%	0.000	0.371
601-620	77	63	0.04%	0.02%	0.000	0.624
581-600	72	67	0.03%	0.02%	0.000	0.710
561-580	106	75	0.05%	0.03%	0.000	0.540
541-560	116	97	0.06%	0.04%	0.000	0.638
521-540	153	121	0.07%	0.04%	0.000	0.603
501-520	156	221	0.07%	0.08%	0.000	1.081
481-500	201	208	0.10%	0.08%	0.000	0.789
461-480	231	293	0.11%	0.11%	0.000	0.968
441-460	238	363	0.11%	0.13%	0.000	1.163
421-440	305	438	0.14%	0.16%	0.000	1.095
401-420	360	547	0.17%	0.20%	0.000	1.159
381-400	419	629	0.20%	0.23%	0.000	1.145
361-380	466	856	0.22%	0.31%	0.001	1.401
341-360	568	986	0.27%	0.36%	0.001	1.324
321-340	598	1123	0.28%	0.41%	0.001	1.433
301-320	768	1326	0.37%	0.48%	0.001	1.317
281-300	867	1790	0.41%	0.65%	0.002	1.575
261-280	1112	2212	0.53%	0.80%	0.003	1.517
241-260	1368	2773	0.65%	1.01%	0.004	1.546
221-240	1797	3740	0.85%	1.36%	0.005	1.588
201-220	2102	8025	1.00%	2.91%	0.019	2.912
181-200	2543	6499	1.21%	2.36%	0.011	1.949
161-180	3427	13690	1.63%	4.96%	0.033	3.047
141-160	3929	11337	1.87%	4.11%	0.022	2.201
121-140	5316	15954	2.53%	5.79%	0.033	2.289
101-120	7565	20691	3.60%	7.50%	0.039	2.086
81-100	12093	27752	5.75%	10.06%	0.043	1.751
61-80	19312	40755	9.18%	14.78%	0.056	1.610
41-60	31472	52191	14.96%	18.93%	0.040	1.265
21-40	56590	50538	26.90%	18.33%	-0.086	0.681
0-20	55679	10260	26.47%	3.72%	-0.227	0.141

Table 11: Population Stability Distribution from Portfolio1 part 2

Final Score Interval	LN(A7)	Contribution to Index [A8*A6]	Ascending Cum %.A5	Ascending Cum %.A4
A1	A8	A9	A10	A11
641+	-1.163	0.001	0.04%	0.13%
621-640	-0.991	0.000	0.06%	0.17%
601-620	-0.471	0.000	0.08%	0.21%
581-600	-0.343	0.000	0.10%	0.24%
561-580	-0.617	0.000	0.13%	0.29%
541-560	-0.450	0.000	0.16%	0.35%
521-540	-0.505	0.000	0.21%	0.42%
501-520	0.078	0.000	0.29%	0.49%
481-500	-0.237	0.000	0.36%	0.59%
461-480	-0.033	0.000	0.47%	0.70%
441-460	0.151	0.000	0.60%	0.81%
421-440	0.091	0.000	0.76%	0.96%
401-420	0.148	0.000	0.96%	1.13%
381-400	0.136	0.000	1.19%	1.33%
361-380	0.337	0.000	1.50%	1.55%
341-360	0.281	0.000	1.86%	1.82%
321-340	0.359	0.000	2.26%	2.10%
301-320	0.275	0.000	2.74%	2.47%
281-300	0.454	0.001	3.39%	2.88%
261-280	0.417	0.001	4.19%	3.41%
241-260	0.436	0.002	5.20%	4.06%
221-240	0.462	0.002	6.56%	4.91%
201-220	1.069	0.020	9.47%	5.91%
181-200	0.668	0.008	11.82%	7.12%
161-180	1.114	0.037	16.79%	8.75%
141-160	0.789	0.018	20.90%	10.62%
121-140	0.828	0.027	26.68%	13.14%
101-120	0.735	0.029	34.19%	16.74%
81-100	0.560	0.024	44.25%	22.49%
61-80	0.476	0.027	59.03%	31.67%
41-60	0.235	0.009	77.95%	46.63%
21-40	-0.384	0.033	96.28%	73.53%
0-20	-1.962	0.446	100.00%	100.00%

Note: Population Stability Index (sum of contribution): 0.687

The Characteristics Analysis results are presented in Table 8. The Characteristic Analysis reveals that statistically significant changes in the characteristics have occurred since the development for some of the attributes. The attributes with the most noticeable shifting distributions are: DM Account Count, Initial LOC Limit, Account Average Overlimit Amount in the Last 6 Months, and Number of Accounts in DM in the Last 6 Months. Several positive changes have occurred on the portfolio. For example, the Average 30 days Delinquent Amount in the last 6 months has decreased slightly. As well, the Account Average Overlimit Amount in the last 6 months and the Trades Ever 90 days or Derogatory have decreased indicating that positive steps have been taken in addressing delinquent accounts. The initial LOC limit (DM) has increased since 2002 development. In general, this is likely reflective of our customers increasing appetite for credit. Finally, the variable Number of Accounts in DM in last 6 months has changed dramatically. A shift has occurred in the distribution of the data, the number of customers with 1-2 accounts in DM in the past 6 months has increased by 71%.

P2 accounts are expected to stay in the collections queues longer because P2 accounts score higher. P2 accounts with a longer expected window of delinquency will be treated with a more expensive collection remedy (i.e. a phone call vs. a letter). Collection activities may become less efficient.

It appears from this analysis that further investigation is called for to determine the source of this change the strategy team and IT to identify how the attribute has changed. This investigation would need participation from the model development team, the strategy team and IT. Overall, the models continue to rank-order well (KS = 44.4) but there is some evidence of natural aging.

10.5 Conclusions

Risk in an enterprise can be quantified and managed using various models. Models also provide support to organizations seeking to control enterprise risk. ERM provides tools to integrate enterprise-wide operations and finance functions. The promise of ERM lies in allowing managers to better understand and use their firms' fundamental relation to uncertainty in a scientific framework: from each risk, strategy may create opportunity. We have discussed risk modeling and reviewed some common risk measures. We have demonstrated how different risk measures in ERM acts to integrate operation and finance functions. Using the variation of these measures, we demonstrate support to risk management through validation of predictive scorecards for a large bank.

Credit scoring is an important finance operation activity in financial service industry, focusing on financial risk forecasting to consumer lending. It has mainly been used as a tool to forecast future bad debt in order to set aside appropriate provisioning. Similar models are also used in non- financial service industry, using the concept of 'reject inference.'[4] What firms do seems to depend as much on the culture of the organisation as on any statistical validation. Thomas identified non-financial firms such as retailers and mail order firms tend to accept all applicants for a short period of time and use that group to build scorecards, while a financial services firm are swayed by the cost of default and can never accept everyone, even for a trial, and so use versions of reject inference.[5] A variation of scoring models is made between scoring for default and scoring for targeting potential sales. Thus, the scoring models can be used to forecast product sales and the profit a firm will make in the future, providing a great deal of support to various operations decisions.

Endnotes

1. Sobehart, J., Keenan, S. (2001). Measuring Default Accurately, *Credit Risk Special Report, Risk* 14, 31–33.
2. Thomas, L. C. (2000). A survey of credit and behavioural scoring: forecasting financial risk of lending to consumers. *International Journal of Forecasting*, 16: 2149–172.
3. Note that all time has been modified in order to protect proprietarial interests.

4. Reichert, A. K., Cho, C.-C., Wagner, G. M. (1983). An examination of the conceptual issues involved in developing credit scoring models. *Journal of Business and Economic Statistics* 1, 101–114; Joanes, D. N. (1993). Reject inference applied to logistic regression for credit scoring. *IMA Journal of Mathematics Applied in Business and Industry* 5, 35–43.
5. Thomas (2000), op cit.

PART III: Cases

Chapter 11

Hydro One Financial Risk

Relates experiences of a firm in establishing enterprise risk
  management
Demonstrates ERM framework and policies
Describes the risk assessment process used
Discusses aspects of risk appetite and how it was established at
  Hydro One
Describes measures used

Hydro One Inc. is the largest provider of electricity in Ontario Province in Canada. Hydro One is responsible to build transmission lines to municipal utilities from power generated at Niagara Falls. It consists of three businesses, one responsible for transmission, one for distribution, one for telecommunications. The vast majority of its business comes from transportation of electricity through the high-voltage provincial grid and low-voltage distribution to municipal utilities, large industrial customers, and over one million individual users. Hydro One has about 4 thousand employees. All shares in Hydro One are owned by the Ontario government.[1]

In 2001, the Ontario government announced that it was proceeding with an initial public offering (IPO). However, this move was challenged in court, and the prospectus was withdrawn. Hydro One obtains long-term financing from debt markets, and short-term liquidity from commercial paper.

At the time of its original formation in 1999, the management and board of Hydro One set high goals for being a best-practices organization with superior corporate governance and business conduct. Enterprise risk management was established that year. The firm wanted to look at risks and opportunities in an integrated way with hopes of obtaining better overall allocation of corporate resources. New external challenges existed due to the scheduled deregulation of electricity markets. Increased corporate governance scrutiny called for a comprehensive risk management program.

11.1 Initial Risk Management Organization

Initial risk management efforts were led by external consultants, but Hydro One saw no lasting benefits from this initiative. In late 1999, the Head of Internal Audit at Hydro One was appointed Chief Risk Officer (CRO). A Corporate Risk Management Group was established, consisting of the CRO supported by two full-time professionals, one with an MBA in process reengineering and organizational effectiveness, the other an industrial engineer. This group was given six months to prove their worth. If results were not forthcoming at that time, enterprise risk management would be abandoned at Hydro One.

Early in 2000 this group prepared an ERM policy and an ERM Framework. The policy set forth governing principles and assigned responsibility for specific risk management activities. Figure 1 extracts the governance structure outlined in the ERM policy. The framework set out ERM procedures in more detail. These documents were presented to the Executive Risk Committee, which included the CEO. The Executive Risk Committee suggested a pilot study applied to a small subsidiary before formal approval was granted.

The **Audit & Finance Committee** of the Board reviews annually with the officers of the Corporation: the Corporation's risk profile, the risk retention philosophy/risk tolerances of the Corporation, and the risk management policies, processes and accountabilities within the corporation.

The **President** has ultimate accountability for managing the Corporation's risks. The **Chief Financial Officer** has specific accountability for ensuring that enterprise risk management processes are established, properly documented and maintained by the Corporation.

The **Senior Management Team** provides management oversight of the Hydro One risk portfolio and the Corporation's risk management processes. It provides direction on the evaluation of these processes and identifies priority areas of focus for risk assessment and mitigation planning.

Each of the **President's Direct Reports** has specific accountabilities for managing risks in their subsidiary or function. Each will establish specific risk tolerances for their lines of business that do not exceed the limits of corporate risk tolerances. On an annual basis, each is also expected to formally attest that the unit's risk management process is in place, operating effectively and is consistent with this policy.

Line and Functional Managers are responsible for managing risks within the scope of their authority and accountability. Risk acceptance or mitigation decisions will be made explicitly and within the risk tolerances specified by the head of the subsidiary or function.

The **Chief Risk Officer** provides support to the President, CFO, Senior Management Team and key managers within the corporation. This support includes developing risk management policies, frameworks and processes, introducing and promoting new techniques, preparing annual corporate risk profiles, maintaining a registry of key business risks, and facilitating risk assessments across the Corporation.

Figure 1: Hydro One Responsibilities and Accountabilities

The ERM Framework is sketched in Figure 2:

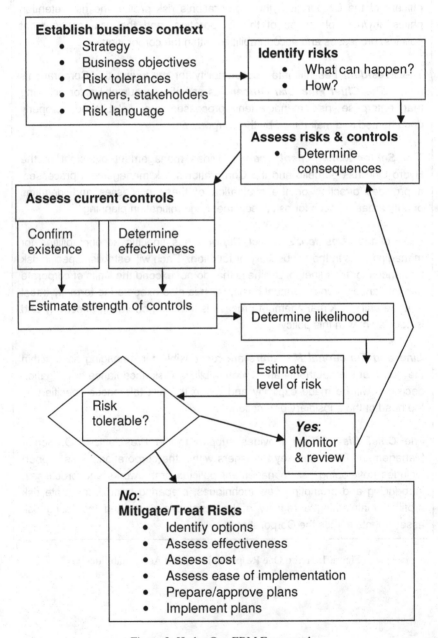

Figure 2: Hydro One ERM Framework

11.2 Risk Tolerance

Risk tolerance definitions were categorized by level. **Minor** risks were noticeable but manageable. **Moderate** risks involved material deterioration in performance, calling for management consideration. **Major** risks involved significant deterioration in performance that were not acceptable, calling for managerial response. **Severe** risks were fundamental threats to operating results, calling for immediate senior management attention. The **worst case** risks threatened company survival in its current form, with potential full-time senior management response required until resolution. Risk tolerance definitions for three of the sixteen risks identified at Hydro One are given in Table 1.

11.3 Pilot Study

The Corporate Risk Management Group, aided by consultants, prepared an ERM workshop in the selected subsidiary, which was delivered in Spring 2000. A list of about 80 potential risks or threats was developed and e-mailed to the subsidiary's management team. Each of these management team members was asked to select the ten most critical risks facing the company. Based on this input, the eight highest ranked were selected for discussion at the workshop. After discussion by the management team, relative importance of these eight risks was obtained by the Delphi method, yielding a prioritized list of risks based on magnitude, probability, and quality of controls available.

The Delphi method[2] consists of distributing issues to participants and obtaining their individual inputs, then sharing these inputs among all participants anonymously. After reading the other inputs, each participant reassesses their views and writes a new report. These inputs are again compiled for the group and shared anonymously. This process interates either a predetermined number of cycles (for instance, three), or until some convergence is obtained, or until the process administrators feel that progress has ceased. It is considered to be quite effective at forecasting in environments where little objective data is available. The core idea of the Delphi method is obtaining subjective expert consensus. The Nominal Group Technique is quite similar, differing primarily in that it does not include anonymity.

Table 1: Hydro One Risk Tolerances

	Financial	**Reputation**	**System Reliability**
Event impact	Net income shortfall (one year, after tax)	Negative media, opinion leaders, public criticism	System outages: ANY of the following
1 Minor	<$5 million shortfall	Letter to Government or senior management	<1000 customers <10MW for <4 hours Near threshold for one NERC standards
2 Moderate	$5 to $25 million shortfall	Local profile	1000-10000 k customers 10-100 MW for 4-24 hours Near threshold for many NERC standards
3 Major	$25 to $75 million shortfall	Provincial profile; Several visible criticisms	10000-40000 k customers 100-400 MW for 2-4 days NERC expression of concern
4 Severe	$75 to $150 million shortfall	National media; Most visible critics	40000 to 100000 k customers 400-1000 MW for 4-7 days Failure to meet minimum standards
5 Worst Case	>$150 million shortfall	International media; Near unanimous critics	>100000 customers >1000 MW for > 7 days Failure to meet NERC minimum standards

The first vote in the pilot study concerned perceived magnitude of the risk in question using a five point scale: {minor, moderate, major, severe, worst case}. The initial vote for each risk was discussed, focusing on definition, causes, and consequences. If high dispersion in opinions existed, the discussion was longer. After discussion, a second vote was taken followed by further discussion until a clear alignment or identifiable cause of disagreement was established. Usually no more than three votes were needed. After this discussion, preliminary action plans were discussed and specific managers identified as champions with responsibility for developing more concrete action plans.

The process was deemed valuable, allaying concerns of some risks, identifying new risks, and reaching common understanding of risks and how they fit into the corporate plan to manage risks. Participants were asked to rate the quality and benefits of the workshop, giving high ratings. The pilot study was considered successful, was presented to the board, and the Audit and Finance Committee of Hydro One's board approved the ERM Policy and ERM Framework in the summer of 2000.

11.4 The Business Context of Risk Management at Hydro One

Hydro One's overall aim was not risk elimination or risk reduction, but rather attaining an optimal balance between business risks and business returns. Figure 3 repeats risk definitions given in Hydro One's Risk Management policy.

Risks were identified, and then assessed on dimensions of likelihood and magnitude, as well as on a scale of management ability to manage that risk. To further aid shared understanding, Hydro One established a common probability rating 1-5 scale (applying fuzzy principles converting numbers to semantic categories):

- 5 – **Virtually certain**: 0.95probability event will occur within 5 years;
- 4 – **Very likely**: 0.75 probability event will occur within 5 years;
- 3 – **Even odds**: 0.50 probability event will occur within 5 years;
- 2 – **Unlikely**: 0.25 probability event will occur within 5 years;
- 1 – **Remote**: 0.05 probability event will occur within 5 years.

Risk: the potential that an event, action or inaction will threaten Hydro One's ability to achieve its business objectives. Risk is described in terms of its likelihood of occurrence and potential impact or magnitude. Broad categories of risk in Hydro One include strategic, financial, and operational risks.

Risk Assessment: The systematic identification and measurement of business risks on a project, line of business or corporate basis. It also includes the review or establishment of risk tolerances, the evaluation of existing mitigation controls and conscious acceptance or treatment of residual risk.

Risk Mitigation/Treatment: Actions or decisions by management that will change the status of a risk. Options include retaining the risk (either completely or partially), increasing the risk (where mitigation is not cost-effective), avoiding the risk (by withdrawing from or ceasing the activity), reducing the likelihood (by increasing preventive controls), reducing the consequences (by emergency or crisis response), and/or transferring the risk (by outsourcing, insurance, etc.).

Risk Profile: The results of any risk assessment, assembled into a consolidated view of the significant strategic, regulatory, financial and operational risks at play in a project, line of business or across the Corporation.

Risk Tolerances: Guidelines first establish levels of acceptable and unacceptable exposure from any risk. Tolerances define the range of possible impacts (from minor to catastrophic) that risks might have on business objectives. Risk tolerances are established for the Corporation and reviewed annually. Each project, function or line of business assessing its risks is expected to use or develop a set of risk tolerances that does not exceed established corporate limits.

Figure 3: Hydro One ERM Policy Definitions

As stated earlier, the scale for risk magnitude also included five categories. Each of these magnitudes had a corresponding strength of control:

1. Minor risk magnitude – few controls needed;
2. Moderate risk magnitude;
3. Major risk magnitude

4. Severe risk magnitude
5. Worst case risk magnitude – full prescriptive controls with executive oversight.

11.4.1 *Hydro One risk tolerance*

Each risk owner (manager responsible for an identified risk) determined the firm's tolerance for that specific risk. Given the risk owner's accountability, the manager would decide to accept the risk as it was or to take steps to mitigate that risk. For risks that were accepted, monitoring and review were applied. Thus the optional means of dealing with a risk was selected from the following seven levels:

- **Retain** – risk exposure accepted without mitigation, since potential return is viewed as desirable and downside exposure is not significant;
- **Retain but change mitigation** – a partially mitigated exposure is maintained, but change in mitigation reduces the cost of control;
- **Increase** – risk exposure is increased, either because the potential return is viewed as desirable or the controls in place are not cost effective;
- **Avoid** – risk exposure to be entirely eliminated, possibly by withdrawal from a business area, since the potential return does not offset downside exposure;
- **Reduce the likelihood** – risk exposure reduced cost-effectively through new or enhanced preventive controls;
- **Reduce the consequences** – the impact of any risk that materializes will be reduced through emergency preparedness or crisis response;

Changes in risk tolerances can occur. Hydro One had decided to issue shares on the New York Stock Exchange. In the period prior to IPO, one of management's greatest fears was the possibility of negative news stories in the international press. As it happened, the IPO was cancelled. In October 2003, the company had an oil spill releasing toxic material into a small stream and received negative press in Ontario. This gained attention from the Ontario Government, Hydro One's shareholder. The

Board of Directors and Corporate Risk Management Group quickly realized that their greatest reputational exposure was not international press, but rather local press and their ability to influence Hydro One's primary stakeholder. Other changes in the risk magnitude for risks from various sources also occurred over time. Hydro One's eleven greatest perceived risks are given in Table 2:

Table 2: Corporate Risk Profile for Hydro One

Risk Source	Rating Dec 1999	Rating June 2000	Trend	Mitigation
Growth	Very high	Very high	Up	Senior management participation in government review processes; planning & analysis, staff skill development, external advisors
Regulatory uncertainty	Very high	Very high	Up	More effective interactions with regulatory boards, add senior regulatory staff
Organizational readiness	High	High	Up	Performance contracting, labor relations, improved technology
Network services subsidiary launch	n/a	High	New	Strategy and transition plan
Asset condition	High	High	Even	Transmission redundancy, emergency response development
Catastrophic events	High	High	Down	Emergency preparedness planning, weather forecasting, insurance
Environmental contamination	High	High	Even	Limited insurance coverage
Hazardous operating environment	Medium	Medium	Up	Facilities design, asset maintenance, safe practices, training & supervision
Market ready project	Medium	Medium	Even	High priority & profile; Market opening delay reduced risk
New electricity marketplace	Medium	Medium	Even	Participation on market board, negotiating operating agreement
Economy / financial markets	Medium	Medium	Down	Limiting floating rate debt, interest rate swaps, diversified customer base

11.4.2 *Risk treatment investment planning*

For specific projects to mitigate risk, a methodology was developed to quantify analysis. For those risks classified as intolerable, funding was provided to mitigate. For risks with lower rated risk intensities, financial analysis was conducted with the intent of estimating expected return in terms of "bang for the buck" designed to provide an index in terms of risk reduction per dollar spent. The index in essence was risk reduced divided by cost. Risk reduction projects were ranked by this index. When cumulative expenditures reached the level of available resources, project funding ceased for that year's plan. This input was provided to those participating in a two-day meeting of senior asset managers and executives, who inquired into assumptions before the Board of Directors was given the investment plan.

11.5 ERM Outcomes and Benefits at Hydro One

Hydro One claimed a number of benefits from their ERM program. The enterprise-wide approach was credited with providing management of regulatory, strategic, operational, and financial risks in alignment with strategic business objectives. Financially, credit rating agencies had positive reactions to the program, leading to reduction in the company's cost of debt to include a higher rating than initially anticipated. Specific benefits are reviewed:

- **Lower debt cost**: Initial debt issue was oversubscribed about 50 percent, and ERM was credited by ratings analysts as being a significant factor in high ratings received by Hydro One.
- **Capital expenditures focused on greatest risk mitigation per investment**: the risk-based structural approach yielded an optimal portfolio of capital investments. The method was also applied to 88 corporate utility acquisitions during 2000, and to proposal to build underground cable to the U.S.
- **Catastrophe avoidance**: Many unusual events occurred since adopting ERM. Two significant risk events were spelled out in the Corporate Risk Tolerances ahead of time. These were the dismissal of the Board of Directors and reaction to the oil spill.

- **Reassurance to stakeholders that the business is well managed**: During IPO presentations, ERM workshops aided the executive team to articulate risks faced. Many other examples of stakeholder reassurance existed.
- **Improve corporate governance**: The Board of Directors was initially skeptical, but now routinely expects risk analysis. Directors recognize that Hydro One is more advanced in ERM than the other companies they represent.
- **Implement formalized risk management system**: The formalized system drives periodic assessment, documentation, and risk reporting.
- **Identify risks where Hydro One is most competitive**: A subsidiary involved in marketing electricity was sold due to high commodity risks; several processing and administrative functions were outsourced to transfer labor union and cost risks.

Aabo et al. reported a five-year experience of implementing enterprise risk management in a Canadian electrical utility. This utility was very successful in this endeavor, leading to the benefits just reviewed. The process reported by Aabo et al. also provides a valuable guideline with concrete implementation examples for other organizations to follow.

Endnotes

1. Aabo, T., Fraser, J.R.S., Simkins, B.J. (2005). The rise and evolution of the Chief Risk Officer: Enterprise risk management at Hydro One, *Journal of Applied Corporate Finance* 17:3, 62-75.
2. Gordon, T.J., Helmer, O. (1964). *Report on a Long Range Forecasting Study* R-2982, Rand Corporation; Woudenberg, F. (1991). An evaluation of Delphi, *Technological Forecasting and Social Change*, September.

Chapter 12

Supply Chain Risk Cases

Discussion of supply chain risks
Description and demonstration of early supplier involvement
Benefits of early supplier involvement obtained at Rolls Royce
Risk of disintermediation to supply chain vendors

This chapter reviews two cases involving risks in supply chains. First, the Rolls Royce experience with early supplier involvement, a procedure designed to reduce some supply chain risk, is reviewed. This is followed by a review of a case reflecting the risk to vendors in participating in supply chains.

Supply chain risk includes the difficulty of coordinating efforts across independent actors. Concurrent engineering has been proposed as a valuable tool in new product development.[1] Thus proactive purchasing organizations seek coordination with critical suppliers through early supplier involvement (ESI) as a means to reach better product, process, and supply chain structure development.[2] Supply risk is the potential of inbound shortages. ESI may also improve supply risk management in the upstream segments of supply chains.[3]

12.1 Early Supplier Involvement

ESI has been defined as a form of vertical cooperation where suppliers participate in product development at the conceptual and design phases of product development.[4] Among the many benefits of ESI are reduced product development time, better product quality, and improved cost. There have been some negative experiences when tasks are improperly sequenced or due to resource shortages. Organizational resistance or incapable suppliers have also caused problems.[5]

The focus of Zsidisin and Smith (2005) was on the impact of ESI on product and supplier failure risk. Failures were defined as quality problems, supplier insolvency, or product introduction delays. Product failure leads to excessive cost, problems with quality, and long lead-times. ESI is expected to reduce supplier failure due to low levels of technological sophistication or leadership, as these characteristics can be supplied in part by the core organization. New product design involves higher risk from technological knowledge, production process capability, quality, and demand uncertainty. ESI involves close working relationships. This can lead to better goal congruity between supplier and purchaser, providing outcome clarity early in product development. Longer term relationships are expected to increase goal alignment. Information systems can serve to better monitor performance needed in ESI. Overall, ESI can shift risk to the supplier through resource and effort requirements.

12.1.1 *Rolls Royce*

Zsidisin and Smith presented a case study involving the Aerospace Division of Rolls Royce. This division was a major supplier of aerospace components for civilian and military aircraft. The industry is characterized by cost and reliability drivers. Extensive research and development is required in developing new products. Rolls Royce typically spent 3 to 4 years to develop a new product, with investments on the scale of one-half billion dollars prior to receiving returns. This contrasted with typical industry product development times of 10 to 20 years.[6] Supplier-provided components represented 65 to 80 percent of Rolls Royce's aerospace products.

About 80 percent of a Rolls Royce product's costs were locked in during the design phase. In 1999 a new purchasing executive was hired. ESI was introduced to Rolls Royce at that time, with the intent of reducing costs, leveraging the supply base, improving design, providing better internal documentation of best practices, and managing supply risk.

12.1.2 *ESI process at Rolls Royce*

The ESI process at Rolls Royce consisted of 16 steps:

1. Establish customer need
2. Identify ESI project based on customer needs
3. Develop target costs for components
4. Prepare ESI project and milestones
5. Inform operating business units for participation
6. Determine commodity breakdown
7. Develop potential supplier list
8. Develop business objective and ESI package
9. Schedule supplier workshops
10. Review workshop expectations with supplier
11. Conduct ESI workshop
12. Conduct value engineering, evaluate supplier prices and technical input
13. Conduct supplier evaluation and score by previously established criteria
14. Make supplier recommendations
15. Inform suppliers
16. Develop working agreements and implement plan

Zsidisin and Smith interviewed six Rolls Royce managers. ESI enabled supply risk reduction in a number of areas, to include:

- Threat of excessive costs,
- Legal liabilities,
- Quality problems,
- Supplier capacity constraints,
- Extended product development times,
- Inability to handle product design changes,
- Supplier organizational leadership issues.

Excessive cost reduction was the major driver for Rolls Royce. Prior to ESI, management felt that they were being priced out of an increasingly competitive market. World class suppliers were expected to have cost reduction programs in place, while less competent suppliers were not. Thus target costing was a major component of Rolls Royce's ESI, and if costs reduction programs were not in place, Rolls Royce would help suppliers develop these programs. With time, Rolls Royce identified a cadre of qualified suppliers and a process to working with them to reduce costs.

Legal liability represented a significant potential risk in product development. Liability depends on which party has critical expertise. Sharing of expertise reduces risk of product failure. Agreements providing for gain sharing reduced potential risks from intellectual property rights concerns. ESI was found to decrease the chance of legal liability issues, as well as the resulting loss should they occur.

Quality problems can be resolved by alignment of designs and capabilities early in the design cycle. Concurrent design engineering ensures resolutioin of design problems that would otherwise lead to extensive rework and yield problems. Use of scorecards records data about supplier performance. Rolls Royce continuously monitored current supplier performance, and used that information to select suppliers for future projects. This reduced the risk associated with quality problems.

Supplier capacity constraints can hamper supplier flexibility. Rolls Royce engaged suppliers during the preselection process to discuss their planning process, previous growth, current status, and investments to improve capacity. Rolls Royce found that this led to better management of the risk of capacity constraints even during economic downturns. ESI information sharing provided value in determining the adequacy of supplier capacity planning and providing the supplier with information leading to better planning for future requirements.

Extended product development times lead to high risk of cost increase and delivery delays. ESI provided risk reduction through shared development information, leading to early recognition of potential delays, allowing action to mitigate risk through shared resources and possible material and design changes.

Supplier **inability to handle product design changes** could jeopardize product lines. Rolls Royce found that information exchange through the ESI process helped manage design changes efficiently and effectively because early detection of problems enabled development of more effective alternative strategies.

Supplier organizational leadership problems were easier to identify through ESI. Suppliers were found to readily provide information about their management structures during the initial stages of ESI. One problem that arose for distributed suppliers was that they might have excellent leadership at their central location, but distributed locations might have less effective leadership. In these cases, Rolls Royce had to determine if the potential supplier would be able to rectify deficiencies.

12.2 Vendor Risk

While the last case dealt with risk of supplier failure, this case considers the corresponding risk to suppliers in supply chains. One of the primary impacts of information technology on business has been the opportunity to disintermediate – to gain distribution efficiencies by cutting out middle-men. This leads to greater overall efficiency if middle-men don't offer value that can be provided through technology. For instance, gas stations were a fundamental element in the U.S. economy of the 1970s, providing not only fuel for vehicles, but also personal service and mechanical expertise. These services have been curtailed, as more reliable vehicles and a comprehensive credit card system have led petroleum distribution companies to provide self-service locations for those seeking fuel. Self-service is rarely found, and mechanical expertise is available at dealerships, with independent automobile mechanics having much lower profiles.

Disintermediation has played a strong role in many e-commerce domains, to include music stores, insurance, financial services, and automobile distribution. Mills and Camek (2004) presented a case of Motokov UK Ltd, a European importer/distributor serving the agricultural market (Landini tractors) as well as automobile and tire (Matador Tyre UK) customers.[7] Agricultural machinery (especially tractors) has an industry structure similar to automobiles. Tires are commodities with value added by manufacturer advertising, distributor logistics, and local retailer promotion.

12.2.1 *Landini Tractor operations*

Landini is an Italian agricultural machinery manufacturer marketing
to the U.K. since 1996. It initially dealt with Edwards Ltd, a tractor
dealership. Once a market foothold was established, this arrangement
was terminated in favor of an exclusive (and Landini owned)
importer/distributor. Motokov UK was selected, as they had experience
marketing around 1,000 Zetor tractors per year, and were seen to have
the resources to do the same for Landini. After three and one-half years
of exclusive distributorship, this arrangement was terminated in favor
of a newly formed organization, Landini UK distribution. Thus Landini
first disintermediated Edwards Ltd, and then Motokov, gaining more
direct market access through vertical expansion within their supply
chain.

The loss to the retailers could be significant. Thus there is a need to
have some settlement for damages. In this case, Landini felt that it was
worth settling first with Edwards, second with Motokov, to gain control
over their marketing and distribution. The distributors have motivation
to arrange for long termination notices (ideally years from their
perspective), during which period they would minimize their marketing
and support expenditures to increase their profits prior to contract
expiration. The manufacturer conversely will suffer, and thus is
motivated to negotiate some settlement to enable quick termination.

12.2.2 *Tire operations*

Motokov also dealt in Matador Tyres. Motokov was the exclusive UK
distributor starting in the mid-1990s. Tires have become a frangible
commodity, and margins have dropped to near 5 percent for importers
and 10 percent for manufacturers. These margins are too low for
extensive supply chains. Motokov was disintermediated by Matador in
the early 1990s. In 1994 Motokov made the decision to focus on Czech
Barum tires. Matador was forced to rebuild their business through
alternate supply channels. However, Barum was subsequently acquired
by Continental, who re-configured their supply chain. Motokov ceased
distributing Barum, and returned to Matador in 1995. Motokov was no

longer the sole importer, and the chain was later cut by tight competition and a decision by Matador to feed large distributors.

In 2002 Motokov had a supply chain where hey dealt with distributors as they had in 1995, but also dealt directly with a set of major customers. Matador expanded in the UK and gained market share, acquiring some large customers unwilling to deal with distributors who involved extra channel costs. Motokov was too small and expensive to worry Matador, and was disintermediated in 2002. They failed to recognize clear signs of risk, and were still readjusting at the time of publication. When the source producer begins to deal directly with customers, intermediate distributors need to understand their vulnerability to disintermediation and minimize their exposure.

12.2.3 *Zetor Tractors*

Zetor was a Czech tractor producer, founded in 1946. In the 1960s they began supplying the U.K. market through Motokov UK. In the late 1990s Zetor suffered financial problems, as they had not made an operating profit in recent times even though they operated at full capacity. Typical of socialist manufacturers, their facilities were widespread. They produced the vast majority of their own components, with a large workforce of over 10 thousand. Production halted gradually over the period 1998 to 2000.

Part of Zetor's financial difficulties came from the rise of input prices coming from participation in the European Union. This eliminated Zetor's traditional price advantage over its competitors. Higher margins and higher sales volume would be required for profitability, which would only be possible through a more efficient supply chain. Zetor also had a change in ownership.

Motokov UK had a volume of around 600 Zetor tractors per year prior to 1998. After production at Zetor was curtailed, this dropped to about 200 tractors per year. Zetor would have benefited from buying out the Motokov UK franchise, giving them cost reductions that might have enabled them to continue operations. Motokov would have benefited from such a buyout as well, because if Zetor did not improve its profitability, it would not be able to supply tractors to Motokov UK anyway. Had that option been taken, Motokov UK would have had to carefully plan the divestment through advance stock reduction.

12.3 Conclusions

ESI enabled longer term relationships and closer coordination, which allowed implementation of more systematic standards leading to lower costs. ESI included effective sharing of expertise, and sharing of monitoring measurements. Demand forecasts were also shared immediately to improve planning.

Specifically, Zsisidin and Smith expected reduction of uncertainty to lead to reduction of product failure, which in turn led to improved cost reduction and product design lead-time reduction. Supplier failure reduction was expected from coordinated programming and monitory, from goal congruency, from adverse selection hazards, and from allowing purchasing firms to better monitor supplier activities. Reducing supplier failure was expected to lead to better quality performance, better technological expertise development, and better leadership.

Proper supplier selection was obtained through an exhaustive selection process. Comprehensive information exchange was helpful in developing better relationships with suppliers, which Rolls Royce found reduced supply risk.

The Motokov UK case demonstrates the risks from disintermediation from supply chain distributors. Motokov UK suffered two disintermediations and was faced with a third. While participation in supply chains can be very beneficial to its participants, it does involve risks. Distributors as well as core supply chain organizations need to manage their risks. To do business with Wal-Mart, vendors have to spend a great deal to develop compatible information sharing systems. Some firms, such as Vlasik Pickles and Snapper Lawn Mowers, have not found the cost to be worth the benefit.[8] There will be risks in just about any business activity. The key is to accept those which the organization can profitably manage.

Endnotes

1. Koufteros, X.A., Vonderembse, M.A., Doll, W.J. (2002). Concurrent engineering and its consequences, *Journal of Operations Management* 19:1, 97-115; Gerwin, D, Barrowman, N.J. (2002). An evaluation of research on integrated product development, *Management Science* 48:7, 938-953.
2. Wynstra, F., VanWeele, FA., Weggemann, M. (2001). Managing supplier involvement in product development: Three critical issues, *European Management Journal* 19:2, 157-167; Millson, M.R., Wilemon, D. (2002). The impact of organizational integration and product development proficiency on market success, *Industrial Marketing Management* 31:1, 1-23.
3. Zsidisin, G.A., Smith, M.E. (2005). Managing supply risk with early supplier involvement: A case study and research propositions, *The Journal of Supply Chain Management* Fall, 44-56.
4. Dault, F., Despres, C., Butler, C. (1998). New product development and early supplier involvement (ESI): The drivers of ESI adoption, *International Journal of Technology Management* 15:1/2, 49-69.
5. Zsidisin and Smith (2005), op cit.
6. Fine, C.H. (1998). *Clockspeed: Winning Industry Control in the Age of Temporary Advantage* Reading, MA: Perseus.
7. Mills, J.F., Camek, V. (2004). The risks, threats and opportunities of disintermediation, *International Journal of Physical Distribution & Logistics Management* 34:9, 714-727.
8. Fishman, C. (2006). *The Wal-Mart Effect*. New York: Penguin Books.

Chapter 13

ERP Risk Cases

Describes benefits and risks of enterprise resource planning (ERP)
  systems
Reviews a well-known ERP implementation failure
Reviews two reported successful implementations of ERP
Infers factors that were credited with making successful ERP
  implementations work

ERP has become a major software product line. An idea started by SAP
in the early 1970s has evolved into a major information system software
product line, which has revolutionized how many large organizations
approach business computing. Sales figures are widely available on the
web, but these sources are usually based upon marketing literature, with
less than complete accuracy. However, the basic picture is clear. Initial
arguments were for completely integrated systems, yet vendors usually
made sales in the form of modules, covering only limited functions of a
business's computing needs. This was because companies usually were
concerned with the high price tags involved, and apparently wanted to
minimize their risks by trying out part of the ERP system. ERP vendor
sales peaked in the late 1990s, driven in part by concerns about Y2K
problems. This induced many large organizations to adopt ERP as a way
to kill two birds with one stone – cleaning up and integrating their
organizational computing services at the same time that they assured
themselves that they would be Y2K compliant. After that pre-Y2K rush,
sales dropped. Vendors then shifted gears, seeking to fill in missing
modules in large company systems, and developing products more
attractive to small to mid-sized firms. Additionally, vendors have made

great strides in reducing some of the trauma of implementing an ERP, making it possible to implement systems much faster (a matter of months rather than years), and offering more sophisticated functionality, such as customer relationship management and e-business system support. Furthermore, ERP is being marketed heavily in nonprofit sectors, to include both government and educational sectors. The prosperity of ERP vendors is a matter of dispute. The market for this product does not appear to have recovered its pre-Y2K boom levels, but there still appears to be a viable market. Vendor survival seems to depend on their ability to adapt to new market realities, which will continue to evolve.

A major thrust by ERP vendors since 2000 has been Web portal systems. There have been concerns that this new feature has usually been cosmetic, without true Web-enablement allowing users to access data in real time in mobile environments. To attain such Web-enablement would require replacement of old coding software, which will take years (one estimate is the 2009-2010 time frame).[1]

Regardless, the ERP market has had a major impact on organizations worldwide. ERP vendors have become leaders in software revenue generation. Organizations face major risks because if they do not invest in ERP, they fear that they will not be able to keep up with their competitors with respect to cost efficiency. However, there are many reports of firms going broke (or at least facing financial disaster) because of their efforts to implement ERP. A 2000 report cited only a fraction of ERP implementations to have been completed on time, within budget, and to original specifications.[2] Standish Group reported that over 90 percent of R/3 projects ran late in the late 1990s.[3] Nearly one third of those ERP implementation efforts were abandoned. Root causes were not technology related, but ERP changes the way people do their work, and organizational change needs managing.

This chapter begins with a case of failure. It demonstrates the risks involved in poor project management and planning. There are far more published cases of implementation success, undoubtedly because companies see no value in publicizing problems. We review two ERP implementation cases where there seemed to be success, with discussion of why they seemed to work when most ERP implementations are reported to have failed. The cases emphasize the need for business process reengineering as a means to efficiently implement ERP, and the need for training to show employees how to use the system effectively, and to obtain their support.

13.1 ERP Advantages and Disadvantages

There are many reasons to adopt an ERP. ERP offers an integrated system shared by all users rather than a diverse set of computer applications, which rarely can communicate with each other, and with each having its own set of data and files. ERP provides a means to coordinate information system assets and information flows across the organization. The main benefit is the elimination of sub-organizational silos that focus on their own problems rather than serving the interests of the overall organization. On the downside, ERP systems impose one procedure for the entire organization, which requires everyone to conform to the new system. ERP systems are thus less flexible. But the benefits of integration are usually much greater than the costs of conformity.

Data can be entered once, at the most accurate source, so that all users share the same data. This can be very beneficial, because shared data is used more, by more people, which leads to much more complete and accurate data. As errors are encountered, users demand correction. There are limits, as a set of procedures are needed to seek that changes do not introduce new errors. This makes it harder to make corrections, but again, this added inconvenience is usually well worth the gains of data integration.

ERP systems also can provide better ways of doing things (that's what business process reengineering is about). This idea is the essence of best practices, a key SAP system component. The downside to best practices is that they take a great deal of effort in identifying the best way to proceed with specific business functions, and that they often can involve significant change in how organizational members do their work. Further, as with any theory, what is considered best by one is often not considered best by all.

ERP systems are usually adopted with the expectation that they are going to yield lower computing costs in the long run. Ideally, adopting one common way of doing things is simpler and involves less effort to provide computing support to an organization. In practice, savings are often not realized, due to failure to anticipate all of the detailed nuances of user needs, as well as the inevitable changes in the business environment that call for different best practices and computer system relationships. As we will discuss in Chapter 7, training needs are typically under-budgeted in ERP projects. Furthermore, these training budgets don't usually include the hidden costs of lost productivity as employees cope with complex new systems. Table 1 recaps these pros and cons of ERP systems.

Table 1: ERP Pros and Cons

Factor	Pro	Con
System Integration	Improved understanding across users	Less flexibility
Data Integration	Greater accuracy	Harder to make corrections
Best Practices / BPR	More efficient methods	Imposition of how people do their work Less freedom and creativity
Cost of Computing	More efficient system planned	Changing needs Under-budgeted training expense Hidden costs of implementation

The key rationales for implementing ERP systems are:

- Technology – more powerful, integrated computer systems
  - Greater flexibility
  - Lower IT cost
- Business practices – implementation of better ways of accomplishing tasks
  - Better operational quality
  - Greater productivity

- Strategic – cost advantages can be gained through more efficient systems
  o Improved decision making
  o Support business growth
  o Build external linkages
- Competitive – if an organization's competitors adopt ERP and gain cost efficiencies as well as serve customers better, organizations will be left with declining clientele.
  o Better customer service

13.2 FoxMeyer Drug

One of the most famous cases of ERP implementation was an attempt to strategically gain cost efficiencies through SAP in the 1990s by FoxMeyer Drug. The SAP implementation was claimed as a technical success. However, the overall impact was a spectacular failure, leading to bankruptcy of the adopting firm. The ultimate cause of this failure was subject to debate (in the court system).

FoxMeyer Drug, a holding company in the health care services industry specializing in wholesale distribution of drugs and beauty aids. Their customers were drugstores, chains, hospitals, and care facilities. FoxMeyer had 23 distribution centers across the U.S. Due to an aging population and growth in health care in the U.S., FoxMeyer anticipated high growth in their industry. This industry was characterized by extreme price competition which threatened FoxMeyer's margins. FoxMeyer adopted long-term strategies of efficiently managing inventory, seeking low operating expenses, stronger sales and marketing efforts, and expanded services.

Prior to adoption of SAP, FoxMeyer had three linked data processing centers. Their old system involved customers filling out electronic orders, which were sent to one of their three data processing centers. Orders were filled manually and packaged within 24 hours. The company had recently completed a national distribution center with multiple carousels and automated picking, with the capability of tracking inventory to secondary locations.

The new distribution system was adopted to capitalize on growth. They anticipated large volumes to enable them to lower unit costs, and thus allow them to undercut competitors on price. They hoped to save $40 million or more in annual operating costs.[4] Their new ERP would need to handle hundreds of thousands of transactions, and meet DEA and FDA regulations. SAP's R/3 system was selected, with Andersen Consulting hired to integrate the $65 million system in 1993. At the same time they adopted an $18 million project with another firm to install a warehouse automation system.

The major fundamental error FoxMeyer seems to have committed was to anticipate full savings from their ERP and warehouse based upon timely project completion. They expected their systems to be in place within 18 months. To take full advantage of these anticipated savings, they proceeded to sign large new contracts, underbidding their competitors based upon their new expected lower costs. However, there were coordination problems across systems, as might reasonably have been anticipated. The new contracts that FoxMeyer signed also forced changes in system requirements. Unfortunately, these changes needed to be made after testing and development were underway. As with most IS/IT projects, FoxMeyer's projects were running late. At this time, they lost a key customer to bankruptcy in May 1993, who had accounted for about 15% of their sales. To recover this loss, FoxMeyer signed up a new customer, assuming the immediate cost savings from their ERP. The ERP project was running late with costs escalating to over $100 million. They revised the schedule arbitrarily, telling project management to complete it 90 days earlier than project management thought reasonable.

At the same time, the warehouse system consistently failed, suffering from late orders, incorrect and lost shipments, and losses of over $30 million. In August 1996 FoxMeyer filed for bankruptcy. Subsequently, the firm's assets were purchased by McKesson.[5]

While it is impossible to know exactly why the project went amiss, some issues seem relatively clear. SAP takes the position that their system was successfully installed and functioned appropriately. The apparent factor of concern was an unmerited confidence in the project keeping on schedule, and working as planned. Historically, IS/IT projects tend not to do that. While there are many useful and valuable IS/IT projects, it is only prudent to allow for some slippage in time and budget, and to not count on full project functionality until after testing and installation are complete.

As a follow-up to the FoxMeyer case, a major drug firm (McKesson) purchased some of FoxMeyer's assets, and reported some success. McKesson adopted SAP's R/3 for an initial implementation in the mid-1990s. This project was cancelled in 1996 after spending $15 million. That project had included business process reengineering, but the new processes didn't mesh well with R/3. In 1997, McKesson acquired FoxMeyer Corporation. Based upon their past experiences, McKesson carefully designed a new R/3 implementation project.[6]

The new project was carefully scaled back by dropping a number of modules. The new project was implemented one module at a time to ensure proper functionality. The project management team developed a cautious rollout schedule, and rigorously held to that schedule. A separate group was formed to test the ERP system in order to avoid developer bias. This approach proved successful, in that the final phase of the $50 million system neared on-time completion within budget and without business disruptions.

The system imposed tremendous changes in end user jobs. The implementation project included careful analysis of these changes, with surveys, focus groups, demonstrations, and computer-based training adopted prior to formal training classes. Over 3,000 end users were expected to work on the system by completion of project implementation.

This example demonstrates that it is possible to bring an ERP implementation project in on time, within budget, and with full functionality. There probably is a relation between McKesson's lessons learned from their prior effort, as well as the experience obtained from FoxMeyer Drug. However, as demonstrated by McKesson, such success comes at the cost of a great deal of planning and project management effort.

13.3 Marathon Oil[7]

Marathon Oil Corporation is an integrated energy business involved in exploration and production of crude oil and natural gas. They also are involved in refining, marketing, and transporting. In the late 1990s they had standardized information system platforms for the most part, but were considering an ERP system as a strategic move to make primary financial, human resources, procurement, and reporting processes more cost efficient by integration with technical systems. A cross-functional team was formed to rigorously assess internal business process in their current operations. SAP was the only viable ERP vendor for oil and gas firms in terms of technical and financial capabilities. Marathon conducted a business case considering software functionality and the impact of best practices on their operations. The Marathon team looked at failed efforts by others, applying the principles of the systems failure approach (looking at what went wrong when others tried to do similar things). Top management at Marathon was a strong supporter of the project.

The implementation of the core SAP system began in late 2000, beginning with a new oil and gas revenue accounting system as a pilot test. Plans were to bring 8 modules on line in 13 months. To reduce the risks of implementation, Marathon gave a great deal of attention to the changes in the way their people would do their jobs with the new system. Based on what their experiences as well as what they found out about the experiences of others, Marathon focused on three fundamental drivers of ownership transfer:

- Knowledge transfer – ensuring that employees knew what they were to do under the new system;
- Responsibility transfer – ensuring that employees fully participated in implementing the new system;
- Vision transfer – helping employees use the new tools and processes to gain business efficiencies.

The change management team was proactive as a liaison between project technicians and users. Initial communication focused on informing

Marathon employees of the benefits of the new system. Once understanding was gained, commitment by those employees, which was key to making the new system work, was gained. Initial communications tools included newsletters, a Web site, road shows, town meetings, and visits by key individuals to make employees aware. To ensure understanding, more interactive communication means such as workshops, meetings, conference calls, and collaboration Web sites were used. Even more complex tools were used to gain commitment, to include sandbox systems allowing employees to practice with the new system on developing systems and simulated data.

Marathon was able to meet their schedule of implementation in 13 months. Success was credited to involving skills and gaining commitment of all employees involved, not simply information systems staff. Lessons learned were:

- ERP systems involve much more than software technology. In order to work, the focus needs to be on business functions and processes.
- Strong project management is needed, including detailed planning and execution.
- Employee commitment needs to be gained in order to make the ERP implementation work.
- The firm needs to avoid economizing on implementation team talent.
- Top management support is essential, and needs to be visible.
- Scope creep (modification of the system plan) had to be controlled.
- Customization of the SAP code was minimized.

This successful implementation demonstrates that the high risks involved in implementing an ERP system can be dealt with. However, it needs to be kept in mind that Marathon had many advantages. They began with a relatively centralized system. Further, they did not have major issues with customization. Many organizations implementing ERP have to sacrifice competitive advantages if they do not customize. Customization may be strategically essential. Organizations need to decide whether it is worth the cost, or maybe that ERP is not appropriate for them.

13.4 Pratt & Whitney Canada[8]

Pratt & Whitney Canada is a large aeronautics company with headquarters in Longueuil, Quebec. Competitors include Honeywell, General Electric, and Rolls Royce-Allison, a highly competitive market. Pratt & Whitney's strategy is mass customization, offering products to individual orders at costs matching those of mass production facilities. As part of its competitive strategy, Pratt & Whitney multiplied the number of engine models and cut production times, redesigning their production processes to design to customer specifications with quick and reliable delivery. Pratt & Whitney served customers in ove3r 180 countries, with a network of service centers around the globe.

Customer service requirements called for a shared information system. In June 1996 they began an SAP R/3 implementation, which was completed in January 1999 after two and one-half years. The system was intended to make Pratt & Whitney more agile. Aims were to improve customer response time, reduce work-in-process, increase inventory turnover, and increase visibility of operating costs and inventory.

Options considered included Oracle, BAAN, and SAP. SAP had many successful implementations, and Pratt & Whitney had experience with SAP R/2 systems over the period 1990-1993 (MRP II). The SAP R/3 system was to be a process-based structure integrated across functions. Modules in the R/3 system selected were financial, accounting and controlling, sales and distribution, materials management, production planning, and quality management. An SAP business warehouse was obtained. The system ran at five sites on Hewlett-Packard computers, supported by an Oracle database. This system replaced about 35 legacy systems that were inefficient, costly, slow, and complex R/2 system.[9]

Project planning involved four stages.

- Planning – system planning, benefit analysis, project scoping
- Configuration – architecture, configuration, design, building
- Testing – user training, product testing

- Implementation – switchover to new system, training, documentation.

The SAP fast track methodology was applied. This methodology involved five threads:

1. Project management
2. Technology architecture
3. Process and systems integrity
4. Change management
5. Knowledge transfer

The project team consisted of 345 employees from across the firm, including heavy representation from the company's main processes (sales and distribution, production planning, materials management, finance). There were 168 people in the information technology and change management groups.

Training was emphasized as a knowledge transfer process. Over 100 employees from the six departments most affected were trained to become internal trainers. Pratt & Whitney became a large classroom in 1998, with over 3000 employees taught on both technical issues (navigation and task training) and business-oriented issues (processes and tasks). Over 150 manuals were produced.

The system was implemented using the big bang approach, switching over to the new system at all five sites at one time. This approach is risky, but is usually less expensive should it work. Success was credited to carefully following the plan given in Table 2.

It was decided to implement R/3 with minimal changes. This determined the scope of the project in terms of resources required and thus determined systems to be replaced. It also led to little process reengineering during implementation. Successful cutover to the new system was accomplished on January 4, 1999. In the first month, about 3 thousand calls for assistance were received involving minor matters like passwords, and about 1800 calls for technical difficulties. Of these, 1500 were resolved in the first month. System stability was reached in late January 1999.

Table 2: Pratt & Whitney Total Enterprise System Phases

Phase I	Scoping and planning	Jun – Dec 1996	Defined scope, planned implementation: Evaluated existing processes, identified those needing improvement
Phase II	Determining the level of previous engineering	Jan – Mar 1997	Visioning and targeting: Executives defined their vision of major business processes
Phase III	Process redesign	Apr – Sep 1997	Processes were redesigned. Ten processes were affects, involving 47 sub-processes, and 600 activities.
Phase IV	Configuration	10 months	The new system was configured. The main parameters of each SAP module were determined.
Phase V	Testing and delivery	Aug – Dec 1998	Initial cycle – master file datas Second – static data Third – dynamic data

13.4.1 *Benefits*

Both tangible and intangible benefits were identified. Tangible results included cost avoidance of almost $1 million in year 2000, and increased productivity 11 percent over planned. Receivables were reduced by 6% in terms of days, and ROI was between 30 and 40 percent. Intangible benefits were increased inventory cost visibility, development of an information backbone to support business-process agility, development of support for e-commerce through mySAP.com, and capability to generate future reports using the SAP business warehouse.

13.4.2 *Lessons learned*

Six key lessons learned were noted:[10]

    1. Mounting environmental uncertainty and turbulence created heavy incentive for change. Pratt & Whitney Canada had extensive experience in undertaking changes, such as moving to

just-in-time manufacturing. The capacity to change was attained through organizational values of rigor, efficiency, comparison to best practices, and benchmarking.

2. It was decided to adopt R/3 as it was, without customization, in order to reduce risk. This is not always the appropriate choice for all organizations, but does involve the least risk of implementation project overruns.

3. Rigor, discipline, and expertise were applied in the implementation project. A maximum of over 400 stakeholders from within the company were involved in planning, supported by over 40 external consultants.

4. A culture of results measurement existed, which aided in obtaining operational and measurable objectives, such as improving customer response time, reducing work-in-process, increasing inventory turnover, and reducing inventory and operating costs.

5. Change management was successfully implemented, supported by champions and change agents. This effort was supported by 125 expert users and 4 external change management consultants.

6. Well-planned big bang implementation was accomplished due to careful planning and implementation.

13.5 Conclusions

ERP systems involve heavy tradeoffs for organizational leaders. They can lead to great efficiencies in organizational computing, but they also are extremely expensive. Furthermore, the total costs of an ERP are far greater than the simple software bill. There are consultants to pay, hardware to purchase, and internal personnel on the payroll, and that is just for the installation. One of the major expenses is training, leading to the key direct tradeoff in ERP options. If you adopt a vendor system without modification, as Pratt & Whitney Canada did, that will minimize the complications of the implementation project. But it will MAXIMIZE the changes required in how organizational employees do their jobs. That can be highly expensive, and incredibly unpredictable. Conversely, minimizing impact on how employees do their job would be highly beneficial, but has been found to lead to massive implementation project overruns.

There are many risks associated with ERP systems. There are also competitive risks from NOT adopting an enterprise system. The decision cannot be avoided. Asking SAP or Oracle salespeople will not yield the objective inputs required for rational decision making. Even asking consultants is risky, as their priority is on maximizing their own revenue stream. Sound management cannot avoid the responsibility to study their own situations, and to base their decisions on the soundest data they can obtain.

Endnotes

1. Peloquin, J. (2007). Next generation ERP and the rise of the agile organization, *IT Jungle* 15 Jan 2007, www.itjungle.com/tfh/tfh011507-story03.html.
2. Stapleton, G., Rezak, C.J. (2004). Change management underpins a successful ERP implementation at Marathon Oil, *Journal of Organizational Excellence* 23:4, 15-22.
3. Williamson, M. (1997). From SAP to 'nuts?' *Computerworld* 31:45, Nov. 10, 68-69.
4. Jesitus, J. (1997). Broken promises? FoxMeyer's project was a disaster. Was the company too aggressive or was it misled? *Industry Week* 3 November, 31-37.
5. T. Ehrhart, "Tech lawsuits, insurance costs escalate – as does cost of doing nothing." *National Underwriter* 10, no. 46 (November 12, 2001), pp. 17-20.
6. C. Wilder and S. Davis, "False starts strong finishes," *Information Week* 711 (November 30, 1998), pp. 41-46; C. Stedman, "Flash! ERP works if you're careful," *Computerworld* 33, no. 11 (December 13, 1999), pp. 1, 14.
7. Stapleton and Rezak (2004), op cit.
8. Tchokogué, A., Bareil, C., Duguay, C.R. (2005). Key lessons from the implementation of an ERP at Pratt & Whitney Canada, *International Journal of Production Economics* 95, 151-163.

9. Al-Mashari, M., Zairi, M. (2000). The effective application of SAP R/3: A proposed model of best practice, *Logistics Information Management* 13:3, 156-166.

10. Tchokogué et al. (2005), op cit.

Chapter 14

Training for Natural Disaster Recovery

> Issue: Collocated versus distributed emergency management
> systems
> Communication and information exchange tools used were studied
> The understanding gained was analyzed
> The value of collocated disaster management coordination was
> stressed

This case involved study of a collocated emergency response exercise.[1] It applied information and communication technology in a training context with the aim of improving the effectiveness of emergency management inter-organizational coordination. The research found that there were identifiable advantages to collocation over distributed management. The case considered two interesting utility systems – electricity (a complex system where many parts have to be functioning for the system to operate) and telephones (a simpler system of independent operators). The case demonstrates emergency planning in an environment that is repetitive (crises generated by adverse weather).

14.1 The Problem Event

A major storm hit the western coast of Sweden on 8 January, 2005. Hurricane-force winds blew over many cellular phone masts and power poles, disabling almost all electrical distribution and telephone systems in the region. Uprooted trees made movement to repair these systems difficult.[2] Speedy repair was found problematic, as the utilities involved were unable to effectively work together. The disruption of power and telephone service for several weeks was considered a system failure by the nearly one-half million customers served.

The electrical system was tightly coupled, in that it consisted of many power lines and transfer stations connecting a relatively small number of large, established customers with their customers. The network included few redundancies and electricity is difficult to inventory. Component interactions within the system were complex, making it difficult to identify and isolate failed components. Thus there were ripples of cascading failures crossing company boundaries. This forced rival electrical providers to cooperate in efforts to repair their system. While past weather problems had induced the creation of electricity coordination teams responsible to prepare for extensive power failure across systems, there was difficulty coordinating efforts after the January storm.

The telephone system included a diverse and highly competitive network of mobile telephone and telecom providers, with little incentive to cooperate. Thus it was much easier to identify failed system components and to replace them. This encouraged a more independent disaster planning environment. However, the public sent a clear message that cooperation and preparedness were required. After the January storm, little cooperative effort on the part of telephone companies was observed, probably hampering recovery efforts. After this negative experience, Swedish telecom utilities were forming a cooperative group responsible for telephone system emergency planning.

14.2 Disaster Recovery Training

At issue was the best means of training these disaster recovery teams. The military and civil services constantly train for emergencies. They are expected to deal with any natural or human-induced crisis. But competing utilities have not traditionally had the same focus. Furthermore, disaster planning is often viewed as costly and unnecessary by management. Therefore, convincing and realistic training was required to obtain cooperation among the utility firms involved.

Highly realistic exercises were designed using the information technology tools that would be used in practice. Settings were designed seeking to include as much realism as possible. Collocation was compared with distributed environments. Collocation was expected to result in better communication, more flexible organization capable of reacting more efficiently in a rapidly changing context, development trust, and lead to a more productive working environment.

Swedish electric companies had formulated guidelines for inter-organizational cooperation and coordination. Individual companies were responsible for ensuring sufficient resources to cover potential power failures with minimum impact to Swedish society. A Power Grid Cooperation System using Internet connections displayed the status of the power grid, updated in real time to include calls for repair work, production, and customer use. The system was developed by the electric utility special interest group, who was responsible for maintaining it and making it available throughout Sweden. This system assisted in many of the disaster recovery team's tasks, serving as a tool for planning and supporting emergency management during power failures. It had the ability to register, assess, and distribute information about outages. Since it was accessed over the Web, it assumed electric availability.

A Crisis Information Message System was also created for the purpose of disseminating information to the media and other external parties during emergencies. This system was also Web-based, administered by the Swedish Radio network. It enabled rapid information transfer to the public which was expected to reduce demand on utility company customer service desks.

14.3 The Exercise

An exercise was conducted in real-time, simulating effects similar to the January storm. Hypothetical events were combined with that storm's impact on power and communication systems. The initial intent was to train radio correspondents' crisis communication skills. Some deviance from the actual storm events was credited with making the scenario more realistic for disaster planning. The scenario was played at a training center as well as in parallel at various remote sites. This was a little over three months after the actual storm. The exercise took ten hours, simulating a storm accelerating through the Benelux, Denmark and southern Norway through southwest Sweden moving towards Stockholm. Power outages and downed telephone lines led to severe infrastructure problems.

About 60 people participated. Participants included representatives of the electrical and telecommunications utilities, in addition to other infrastructure organizations and companies. These included decision makers from most companies involved in the real storm responsible for returning service to normal. The electrical coordination team included five representatives of the electrical companies and two from governmental agencies. The participants had extensive domain knowledge, normally working from different locations through telecommunications links. For the exercise, they were collocated, but used the equipment that they were familiar with. A team of telecommunications coordination people did not want to be observed, as this was their first meeting.

The team's task was to coordinate emergency response. This was done by collecting information, assessing situations before and after power failure, distributing resources to the affected area, maintaining contact with responsible government agencies, and obtaining competent people to deal with given situations. The Power Grid Cooperation System (PGCS) was used in the exercise.

Participants included teams of decision makers. A set of two teams were observed operating in two rooms that interacted. These collocated teams had access to whiteboards, computers, telephones, maps, simulated electronic newspapers with exercise information for the days leading up to the exercise, and simulated radio broadcasts. A number of actors were used to play roles of those affected by the simulated disaster. These actors included utility workers, police, firemen, emergency service representatives, and others. Other teams operated through media (telephones, white-boards, the Web) without direct interaction. Data was collected through direct observation, video recording of the team workplace, monitoring of telephones, white-boards, and Internet usage, and semistructured post-exercise interviews of participants.

14.4 Exercise Results

The collocated teams were used to working in a distributed manner, operating from their home offices and coordinating their work through telephone conferences. A meeting location was available for highly critical emergencies, but it had never been used. The teams were skeptical of working at a joint location since their employing utility firms did not want them out of their offices for extended periods.

During the exercise, the collocated teams designated one room as their meeting room, and the other room was used as the hub for telephone and Internet communication. Team members were initially assigned to one or the other room. Meetings were held every hour in the meeting room to listen to radio, share information, and planning. The chairperson coordinated these meetings, and all team members reported. Between meetings, most team members telephoned other teams of decision-makers to exchange information, and discussed issues in subgroups. As the exercise evolved, team members would move between subgroups and rooms. The hallway between rooms became a meeting point and workplace. During periods of low activity, conversation turned to social affairs. The group became more informal over time, with subgroups dynamically changing membership.

A list of seven team functions, with subtasks, were developed based on a published taxonomy of team performance.[3] The use of media in each of these subtasks is given in Table 1.

In Table 1, Continuous was defined as many times per hour, Frequent about once per hour, Occasional several times during the exercise, and Seldom only once or twice during the exercise.

- **Orientation** – involved information exchange about resources, constraints, task goals, and priorities. Internal orientation was between team members, external between team members and other exercise participants.
- **Resource Distribution** – these functions matched team resources to requirements, and balanced workloads. The PGCS and whiteboards were used continuously, with heavy face-to-face communication.

Table 1: Use of Media[4]

Function	White board	Phone	Radio	PGCS	Face-to-Face
Orientation					
a. Internal – resources	****				****
b. Internal – goals	****			****	****
c. Internal – EM resources	****			****	****
d. External – EM resources		****	***		
e. Priority assignment	****				***
Resource Distribution					
a. Assign resources	**			****	***
b. Load balancing	****				***
Timing					
a. General activity pacing	***				***
b. Individual activity pacing	*				***
Response Coordination					
a. Sequencing	**				***
b. Response timing	***				***
Motivational					
a. Performance norming					*
b. Motivating norms					
c. Set team rewards					
d. Reinforce orientation	***				****
e. Balance focus					
f. Internal conflict resolution	***			****	**
g. External conflict resolution		****	*	****	
System Monitoring					
a. General activity	****				***
b. Individual activity					***
c. Adjustment	***				***
Procedure Maintenance					
a. Monitor general procedures					**
b. Monitor individual procedures					
c. Adjust non-standard activities					

* - Seldom; ** - Occasional; *** - Frequent; **** - Continuous
E-mail used occasionally when phone used; Maps used occasionally for Internal coordination of EM resources; Papers used seldom for Internal coordination of EM resources.

- **Timing** – activity timing and pacing was performed frequently, using face-to-face contact and whiteboards.
- **Response Coordination** – sequencing, timing, and resource positioning were accomplished primarily through face-to-face contact, with some use of whiteboards.
- **Motivational** – these activities were reinforcement of task orientation. It was accomplished continuously through face-to-face communication, often aided by whiteboard analysis. The PGCS (and telephone for external contacts) systems were continuously used for resolution of conflicting information, arising from claims from other participants and what the team understood to be the situation. E-mail and radio occasionally were used for purposes of gathering external information.
- **System Monitoring** – monitoring and adjustment of team and individual activities was accomplished through face-to-face and whiteboard contact.
- **Procedure Maintenance** – little activity was observed for this functions, and these only involved how joint responses were to be accomplished. Face-to-face contact served for this function.

Face-to-face and whiteboard communication dominated for the collocated teams. The PGCS was used for emergency management communication both internally and externally, and aided in conflict resolution and resource assignments. Telephone was used heavily for external communication, with e-mail only occasionally being used. Maps and newspapers were not used for much other than internal information exchange concerning the emergency situation. Radio was used more than maps or newspapers, primarily for obtaining information on the external environment.

14.5 Implications

Collocation enables sharing of local context, and allows informal interactions expanding the depth of communications. These features were clearly found beneficial through face-to-face and whiteboard communication.

Woltjier et al. inferred that collocation would be beneficial in developing team trust and common understanding. Collocation enabled interactions that made workload transfer and balancing much more efficient. Technology tools were only found to be of supplemental value. Of the technology tools, the PGCS system provided the greatest support, followed by the telephone.

It is not always possible to collocate emergency management teams. The use of the most popular and effective means of communication (face-to-face and whiteboard) requires collocation. Electronic whiteboards are feasible, to expand the use of information technology to distributed groups. But they don't provide the socialization opportunities that seemed to be useful. Therefore, distributed teams have to cope as best they can. Information technology tools would be of value in providing communication for distributed operations. For internal communications in distributed environments, e-mail and telephone would be much more valuable than they proved in a collocated setting.

Endnotes

1. Woltjer, R., Lindgren, I., Smith, K. (2006). A case study of information and communication technology in emergency management training, *International Journal of Emergency Management* 3:4, 332-347.
2. Alexandersson, H. (2005). Den stora januaristormen 2005, *Väder och Vatten* 1, 11.
3. Fleishman, E.A., Zaccaro, S.J. (1992). Toward a taxonomy of team performance functions, in *Teams: Their Training and Performance*, R.W. Swezey & E. Salas, eds. Norwood, NJ: Ablex Publishing Corporation.
4. Based on table provided by Woltjer, et al. (2006), op cit.

Bibliography

Aabo, T., Fraser, J.R.S., Simkins, B.J. (2005). The rise and evolution of the Chief Risk Officer: Enterprise risk management at Hydro One, *Journal of Applied Corporate Finance* 17:3, 62-75.

Aleskerov, F., Say, A.L., Toker, A., Akin, H.L., Altay, G. (2005). A cluster-based decision support system for estimating earthquake damage and casualties, *Disasters* 3, pp. 255-276.

Alexander, D. (2003). Towards the development of standards in emergency management training and education, *Disaster Prevention and Management* 12, pp. 113-123.

Alexander, G.J., Baptista, A.M. (2004). A comparison of VaR and CVaR constraints on portfolio selection with the mean-variance model. *Management Science* 50(9), pp. 1261-1273.

Alexandersson, H. (2005). Den stora januaristormen 2005, *Väder och Vatten* 1, 11.

Al-Mashari, M., Zairi, M. (2000). The effective application of SAP R/3: A proposed model of best practice, *Logistics Information Management* 13:3, 156-166.

American Institute of Certified Public Accountants, Enterprise risk management — integrated framework, Jersey City, NJ. 2004.

Anders, U., Sandstedt, M. (2003). An operational risk scorecard approach. *Risk* 16:1, pp. 47-50.

Anderson, K. (2007). Convergence: A holistic approach to risk management, *Network Security* May , pp. 4-7.

Antonette, G., Giunipero, L.C., Sawchuk, C. (2002). *E-purchasing Plus: Transforming Supply Management Through Technology*. Goshen, NY: JGC Enterprises.

Ballou, B., Heitger, D.L. (2005). A building-block approach for implementing COSO's enterprise risk management-integrated framework, *Management Accounting Quarterly* 6:2, 1-10.

Balram, S., Dragićević, S. (2006). Modeling collaborative GIS processes using soft systems theory, UML and object oriented design. *Transactions in GIS* 10:2, pp. 199-218.

Banham, R. (2004). Enterprising views of risk management, *Journal of Accountancy* 197:6, pp. 65-71.

Baranoff, E.G. (2004). Risk management: A focus on a more holistic approach three years after September 11, *Journal of Insurance Regulation* 22:4, pp. 71-81.

Barbarosoğlu, G. (2000). An integrated supplier-buyer model for improving supply chain coordination. *Production Planning & Control* 11:8, 732-741.

Barbarosoğlu, G., Yazgaç, T. (2000). A decision support model for customer value assessment and supply quota allocation. *Production Planning & Control* 11:6, 608-616.

Basel Committee on Banking Supervision (February 2003). Sound Practices for the management and Supervision op Operational Risk, Bank for International Settlements.

Basel Committee on Banking Supervision (June 2004). International Convergence of Capital Measurement and Capital Standards, Bank for International Settlements.

Beasley, M., Chen, A., Nunez, K., Wright, L. (2006). Working hand in hand: Balanced scorecards and enterprise risk management. *Strategic Finance* 87:9, pp. 49-55.

Beasley, M.S., Jenkins, J.G., Sawyers, R.B. (2006). Brainstorming to identify and manage tax risks. *The Tax Adviser* 37:3, pp. 158-162.

Bigio, D., Edgeman, R.L., Ferleman, T. (2004). Six sigma availability management of information technology in the Office of the Chief Technology Officer of Washington, DC. *Total Quality Management* 15(5-6), pp. 679-687.

Bowling, B.M., Rieger, L. (2005b). Success factors for implementing enterprise risk management, *Bank Accounting and Finance* 18:3, pp. 21-26.

Bowling, D.M., Rieger, L.A. (2005a). Making sense of COSO's new framework for enterprise risk management, *Bank Accounting and Finance* 18:2, pp. 29-34.

Bresnahan, T.F., Reiss, P.C. (1985). Dealer and manufacturer margins, *Rand Journal of Economics* 16, pp. 253-268.

Bryson, K.M., Sullivan, W.E. (2003). Designing effective incentive-oriented contracts for application service provider hosting of ERP systems. *Business Process Management Journal* 9:6, pp. 705-721.

Buchalter, A.R., Curtis, G.E. (2003). *Inventory and Assessment of Databases Relevant for Social Science Research on Terrorism.* Washington: Federal Research Division, Library of Congress.

Cachon, G., Fisher, M. (2000). Supply chain inventory management and the value of shared information. *Management Science*, 46:8, pp. 1032-1048.

Calandro, J., Jr., Lane, S. (2006). An introduction to the enterprise risk scorecard. *Measuring Business Excellence* 10:3, pp. 31-40.

Callioni, G., de Montros, X., Slagmulder, R., Van Wassenhove, L.N., Wright, L. (2005). Inventory-driven costs. *Harvard Business Review* 82:3, pp. 135-140.

Carnaghan, C. (2006). Business process modeling approaches in the context of process level audit risk assessment: An analysis and comparison, *International Journal of Accounting Information Systems* 7:2, pp. 170-204.

Carr, S., Lovejoy, W. (2000). The inverse newsvendor problem: Choosing an optimal demand portfolio for capacitated resources, *Management Science* 47, pp. 912-927.

Caudle, S. (2005). Homeland security. *Public Performance & Management Review* 28:3, pp. 352-375.

Cetinkaya, S., Lee, C.Y. (2000). Stock replenishment and shipment scheduling for vendor-managed inventory systems, *Management Science* 46:2, pp. 217-232.

Chapman, P., Cristopher, M., Juttner, U., Peck, H., Wilding, R. (2002). Identification and managing supply chain vulnerability, *Logistics and Transportation Focus* 4:4, pp. 59-64.

Chavez-Demoulin, V., Embrechts, P., Nešlehová, J. (2006). Quantitative models for operational risk: Extremes, dependence and aggregation. *Journal of Banking & Finance* 30, pp. 2635-2658.

Checkland, P.B. (1981). *Systems Thinking, Systems Practice.* Chichester, England: John Wiley & Sons.

Chen, F., Federgruen, A., Zheng, Y.S. (2001). Coordination Mechanisms For A Distribution System With One Supplier and Multiple Retailers. *Management Science*, 47:5, pp. 693-708.

Chen, I.J., Paulraj, A. (2004). Understanding supply chain management: Critical research and a theoretical framework. International Journal of Production Research 42:1, 131–163.

Choi, T.Y., Dooley, K.J., Rungtusanatham, M. (2001). Supply networks and complex adaptive systems: Control versus emergence. *Journal of Operations Management* 19, pp. 351-366.

Cilluffo, F.J., Marks, R.A., Salmoiraghi, G.C. (2002). The use and limits of US intelligence, *The Washington Quarterly* 25, pp. 61-74.

Cohen, M.A., Lee, H.L. (1988). Strategic analysis of integrated production–distribution systems: Models and methods. Operations Research 36:2, pp. 216-228.

Cohen Kulp, S. (2002). The effect of information precision and reliability on manufacturer-retailer relationships. *The Accounting Review* 77:3, pp. 653-677.

Committee of Sponsoring Organizations of the Treadway Commission (COSO).

Crook J.N., Edelman, D.B., Thomas, L.C. (2007). Recent developments in consumer credit risk assessment. *European Journal of Operational Research*, 183, pp. 1447-146.

Crouhy, M., Galai, D., Mark, R. (1998). Model Risk, *Journal of Financial Engineering* 7(3/4), pp. 267-288, reprinted in Model Risk: Concepts, Calibration and Pricing, (ed. R. Gibson), *Risk Book*, 2000, 17-31.

Crouhy, M., Galai, D. Mark, R. (2000). A comparative analysis of current credit risk models, *Journal of Banking & Finance* 24, pp. 59-117.

Dalcher, D. (2007). Why the pilot cannot be blamed: A cautionary note about excessive reliance on technology, *International Journal of Risk Assessment and Management* 7:3, pp. 350-366.

Danielson, J., de Vries, C.G. (1997). Extreme returns, tail estimation, and value-at-risk. Working Paper, University of Iceland (http://www.hag.hi.is/~jond/research).

Dault, F., Despres, C., Butler, C. (1998). New product development and early supplier involvement (ESI): The drivers of ESI adoption, *International Journal of Technology Management* 15:1/2, 49-69.

Dearstyne, B.W. (2002). Information and the war on terrorism: Issues and opportunities, *Information Outlook* 6:3, pp. 14-18.

Dekle, J., Lavieri, M.S., Martin, E., Emir-Farinas, H., Francis, R.L. (2005). A Florida county locates disaster recovery centers, *Interfaces* 35:2, pp. 133-139.

Dickinson, G. (2001). Enterprise risk management: Its origins and conceptual foundation, *The Geneva Papers on Risk and Insurance* 26:3, pp. 360-366.

Dickson, G.W. (1966). An analysis of vendor selection systems and decisions, *Journal of Purchasing* 2, pp. 5-17.

Donnellan M., Sutcliff, M. (2006). *CFO Insights: Delivering High Performance*, John Wiley & Sons.

Drew, M. (2007). Information risk management and compliance – Expect the unexpected, *BT Technology Journal* 25:1, pp. 19-29.

Edmiston, A.H. (2007). The role of systems and applications monitoring in operational risk management, *BT Technology Journal* 25:1, pp. 68-78.

Edwards, W. (1977). How to use multiattribute utility measurement for social decisionmaking. *IEEE Transactions on Systems, Man, and Cybernetics* SMC-7:5, pp. 326-340.

Ehrhart, T. (2001), Tech lawsuits, insurance costs escalate – as does cost of doing nothing. *National Underwriter* 10:46 (November 12), pp. 17-20.

Ekanayaka, Y., Currie, W.L., Seltsikas, P. (2003). Evaluating application service providers. *Benchmarking: An International Journal* 10:4, pp. 343-354.

Elsinger, H., Lehar, A., Summer, M. (2006). Risk assessment for banking systems. *Management Science* 52:9, pp. 1301-1314.

Evans, J.R., Olson, D.L. (2002). *Introduction to Simulation and Risk Analysis* 2nd ed.. Upper Saddle River, NJ: Prentice Hall.

Feenberg, A. (1999). *Questioning Technology*, London: Routledge.

Fine, C.H. (1998). *Clockspeed: Winning Industry Control in the Age of Temporary Advantage* Reading, MA: Perseus.

Fisher, M., and Raman, A. (1996). Reducing the cost of demand uncertainty through accurate response to early sales, *Operations Research*, 44:1, pp. 87-99.

Fishman, C. (2006). *The Wal-Mart Effect*. New York: Penguin Books.

Fleishman, E.A., Zaccaro, S.J. (1992). Toward a taxonomy of team performance functions, in *Teams: Their Training and Performance*, R.W. Swezey & E. Salas, eds. Norwood, NJ: Ablex Publishing Corporation.

Fletcher, A.L. (2007). Reinventing the pig: The negotiation of risks and rights in the USA xenotransplantation debate, *International Journal of Risk Assessment and Management* 7:3, pp. 341-349.

Fliedner, G. (2003). CPFR: an emerging supply chain tool, *Industrial Management & Data Systems* 103:1, pp. 14-21.

Florez-Lopez, R. (2007). Modelling of insurers' rating determinants. An application of machine learning techniques and statistical models. *European Journal of Operational Research*, 183, pp. 1488-1512

Fortune, J., Peters, G. (1997). *Learning from Failure: The Systems Approach.* New York: John Wiley & Sons.

Fry, M.J., Kapuscinski, R., Lennon Olsen, T. (2001). Coordinating production and delivery under a (z, Z)-type vendor-managed inventory contract, *Manufacturing & Service Operations Management* 3:2, pp. 151-173.

Garcia, R., Renault, É, Tsafack, G. (2007). Proper conditioning for coherent VaR in portfolio management. *Management Science* 53:3, pp. 483-494.

Garman, M.B. (1996). Improving on VaR. *Risk* 9, No. 5.

Gates, S., Nanes, A. (2006). Incorporating strategic risk into enterprise risk management: A survey of current corporate practice, *Journal of Applied Corporate Finance* 18:4, pp. 81-90.

Gaur, S., Ravindran, A.R. (2006). A bi-criteria model for the inventory aggregation problem under risk pooling. *Computers & Industrial Engineering* 51, 482-501.

Gavirneni, S., Kapuscinski, R., and Tayur, S. (1999). Value of information in capacitated supply chains. *Management Science*, 45:1, pp. 16-24.

Gerwin, D, Barrowman, N.J. (2002). An evaluation of research on integrated product development, *Management Science* 48:7, 938-953.

Gharajedaghi, J. (1999). *Systems Thinking: Managing Chaos and Complexity*, Woburn, MA: Butturworth-Heinemann.

Giunipero, L.C., Aly Eltantawy, R. (2004). Securing the upstream supply chain: A risk management approach, *International Journal of Physical Distribution & Logistics Management* 34:9, pp. 698-713.

Goetschalckx, M., Vidal, C.J., Dogan, K. (2002). Modeling and design of global logistics systems: A review of integrated strategic and tactical models and design algorithms. *European Journal of Operational Research* 143:1, 1–18.

Gordon, T.J., Helmer, O. (1964). *Report on a Long Range Forecasting Study* R-2982, Rand Corporation.

Gorry, G.A. Scott Morton, M.S. (1971). A framework for management information systems, *Sloan Management Review* 13:1, pp. 56-70.

Gramling, A.A., Myers, P.M. (2006). Internal auditing's role in ERM, *Internal Auditor* 63:2, 52-58.

Graves, S.C., Willems, S.P. (2000). Optimizing strategic safety stock placement in supply chains. *Manufacturing & Service Operations Management* 2:1, 68-83.

Gupta, P.P., Thomson, J.C. (2006). Use of COSO 1992 in management reporting on internal control, *Strategic Finance* 88:3, 27-33.

Hale, W.C. (2006). Information versus intelligence: Construction and analysis of an open source relational database of worldwide extremist activity, *International Journal of Emergency Management* 3:4, pp. 280-297.

Hariharan, R., and Zipkin, P. (1995). Customer-order information, lead-times, and inventories, *Management Science*, 41:10, pp. 1599-1607.

Hendricks, K., Singhal, V. (2005). An empirical analysis of the effect of supply chain disruptions on long-run stock price performance and equity risk of the firm, *Production and Operations Management* 14:1, pp. 25-52.

Herath, H.S.B., Bremser, W.G. (2005). Real-option valuation of research and development investments: Implications for performance measurement. *Managerial Auditing Journal* 20:1, pp. 55-72.

Hobbs, B.F., Horn, G.T.F. (1997). Building public confidence in energy planning: A multimethod MCDM approach to demand-side planning at BC Gas. *Energy Policy* 25:3, pp. 356-375.

Holweg, M., Disney, S., Holström, J., Småros, J. (2005). Supply chain collaboration: making sense of the strategy continuum. *European Management Journal*, 23:2, pp. 170-181.

Hull, J.C. (2006). Risk Management and Financial Institutions.

Ireland, R., Bruce, R. (2000). CPFR: only the beginning of collaboration, *Supply Chain Management Review* 4:4, pp. 80-88.

JP Morgan (1996). *RiskMetrics™-technical document,* 4ᵗʰ ed.

JP Morgan (1997). *CreditMetrics™-technical document.*

Jacobson, T., Lindé, J., Roszbach, K. (2006). Internal ratings systems, implied credit risk and the consistency of banks' risk classification policies. *Journal of Banking & Finance* 30, pp. 1899-1926.

Jesitus, J. (1997). Broken promises? FoxMeyer's project was a disaster. Was the company too aggressive or was it misled? *Industry Week* 3 November, 31-37.

Joanes, D. N. (1993). Reject inference applied to logistic regression for credit scoring. *IMA Journal of Mathematics Applied in Business and Industry* 5, 35–43.

Joplin, B., Terry, C. (2000). Financial system outsourcing: The ERP application hosting option. *Government Finance Review* 16(1) pp. 31-33.

Kaipia, R., Holmström, J., Tanskanen, K. (2002). VMI: What are you losing if you let your customer place orders? *Production Planning & Control*, 13:1, pp. 17-25.

Kaplan, R.S., Norton, D.P. (1992). The balanced scorecard – Measures that drive performance. *Harvard Business Review* 70:1, pp. 71-79.

Kaplan, R.S., Norton, D.P. (2006). *Alignment: Using the Balanced Scorecard to Create Corporate Synergies.* Cambridge, MA: Harvard Business School Press Books.

Katz, R. (2005). Tools of the trade: Hunting terrorists, *Crime and Justice International* 20, p. 19.

Keeney, R.L., Raiffa, H, (1976). *Decisions with Multiple Objectives: Preferences and Value Tradeoffs* (New York: John Wiley & Sons).

Khisty, C.J. (1995). Soft-systems methodology as learning and management tool, *Journal of Urban Planning and Development* 121:3, pp. 91-101.

Enterprise Risk Management

Kirkwood, C.W., Slaven, M.P., Maltz, A. (2005). Improving supply-chain-reconfiguration decisions at IBM. *Interfaces* 35:6, 460-473.

Kliem, R.L., Ludin, I.S. (1998). *Reducing Project Risk.* Aldershot, England: Gower.

Koufteros, X.A., Vonderembse, M.A., Doll, W.J. (2002). Concurrent engineering and its consequences, *Journal of Operations Management* 19:1, 97-115.

Kraiselburd, S., Narayanan, V.G., Raman, A. (2004). Contracting in a supply chain with stochastic demand and substitute products, *Production and Operations Management* 13:1, pp. 46-62.

Kremic, T., Tukel, O.I., Rom, W.O. (2006), Outsourcing decision support: A survey of benefits, risks, and decision factors. *Supply Chain Management: An International Journal* 11:6, pp. 467-482.

Kunreuther, H. (1976). Limited knowledge and insurance protection, *Public Policy* 24, pp. 227-261.

Lee, H.L., Billington, C. (1993). Material management in decentralized supply chain. Operations Research 41:5, pp. 835–847.

Levinsohn, A. (2004). How to manage risk – Enterprise-wide, *Strategic Finance* 86(5), pp. 55-56.

Lhabitant, F. (2000). Coping with model risk, in *The Professional Handbook of Financial Risk Management*, M. Lore, L. Borodovsky (eds), Butterworth-Heinemann.

Li, Q. (2007). Risk, risk aversion and the optimal time to produce. *IIE Transactions* 39, 145-158.

Mabert, V.M., Soni, A., Venkataramanan, M.A. (2000). Enterprise resource planning survey of US manufacturing firms. *Production and Inventory Management Journal* 41(20), pp. 52-58.

MacCrimmon, K.R., Wehrung, D.A. (1986). *Taking Risks: The Management of Uncertainty.* New York: Free Press.

Magnusson, C., Olá, H., Holmqvist, C.S. (2006). The knowledge pressure on risk and security managers is increasing. *Proceedings of the First International Conference on Availability, Reliability and Security (ARES'06)*, IEEE Computer Society, 2-0200 April, pp. 974-979.

March, J., Shapira, Z. (1987). Managerial perspectives on risk and risk taking, *Management Science* 33, pp. 1404-1418.

Markel, K.S., Barclay, L.A. (2007). The intersection of risk management and human resources: An illustration using genetic mapping, *International Journal of Risk Assessment and Management* 7:3, pp. 326-340.

Matyjewicz, G., D'Arcangelo, J.R. (2004). Beyond Sarbanes-Oxley, *Internal Auditor* 61:5, 67-72.

McCarthy, T. (2001). Are ASPs for you? *Financial Executive* 17:4, pp. 45-48 (June).

Mentzer, J.T, Dewitt, W., Keebler, J.S., Min, S., Nix, N.W., Smith, C.D., Zacharia, Z.G. (2001). *Supply Chain Management*. Thousand Oaks, CA: Sage.

Mueller, R.S. III (2004). The FBI, *Vital Speeches of the Day* 71:4, pp. 106-109.

Miccolis, J. (2002). Insurers and ERM: Working on the how, *National Underwriter/Property & Casualty Risk & Benefits Management* 107:14, pp. 36-37.

Micheau, V.A. (2005). How Boeing and Alcoa implemented a successful vendor managed inventory program, *The Journal of Business Forecasting*, Spring, pp. 17-19.

Mills, J.F., Camek, V. (2004). The risks, threats and opportunities of disintermediation, *International Journal of Physical Distribution & Logistics Management* 34:9, 714-727.

Millson, M.R., Wilemon, D. (2002). The impact of organizational integration and product development proficiency on market success, *Industrial Marketing Management* 31:1, 1-23.

Moore, C.M. (1994). *Group Techniques for Idea Building* 2nd ed. Thousand Oaks, CA: Sage Publications.

Moskowitz, H., Tang, J., Lam, P. (2000). Distribution of aggregate utility using stochastic elements of additive multiattribute utility models, *Decision Sciences* 31, pp. 327-360.

Narasimhan, R., Talluri, S., Mahapatra, S.K. (2006). Multiproduct, multicriteria model for supplier selection with product life-cycle considerations. *Decision Sciences* 37:4, 577-603.

Ni, D. (2006). Challenges and strategies of transportation modeling and simulation under extreme conditions, *International Journal of Emergency Management* 3:4, pp. 298-312.

O'Donnell, E. (2005). Enterprise risk management: A systems-thinking framework for the event identification phase, *International Journal of Accounting Information Systems* 6:3, pp. 177-195.

Ojala, M., Hallikas, J. (2006). Investment decision-making in supplier networks: Management of risk. *International Journal of Production Economics* 104, 201-213.

Olhager, J., Selldin, E. (2003). Enterprise resource planning survey of Swedish manufacturing firms. *European Journal of Operational Research* 146, pp. 365-373.

Olson, D.L. (1996). *Decision Aids for Selection Problems* (New York: Springer).

Olson, D.L. (2004). *Managerial Issues of Enterprise Resource Planning Systems*. Boston: McGraw-Hill/Irwin.

Papalexandris, A., Ioannou, G., Prastacos, G., Soderquist, K.E. (2005). An integrated methodology for putting the balanced scorecard into action. *European Management Journal* 23:2, pp. 214-227.

Peloquin, J. (2007). Next generation ERP and the rise of the agile organization, *IT Jungle* 15 Jan 2007, www.itjungle.com/tfh/tfh011507-story03.html.

Perrow, C. (1999). *Normal Accidents: Living with High-Risk Technologies*, Princeton, NJ: Princeton University Press, reprinted from 1984.

Pinker, S. (2002). *The Blank Slate: The Modern Denial of Human Nature*. London: Penguin Books.

Porter, M. (1985). *Competitive Advantage*. New York: The Free Press.

Pritsker, M. (1996). Evaluating value at risk methodologies: accuracy versus computational time, unpublished working paper, Board of Governors of the Federal Reserve System

Quinn, L.R. (2006). COSO at a crossroad, *Strategic Finance* 88:1, pp. 42-49.

Rabelo, L., Eskandari, H., Shaalan, T., Helal, M. (2007). Value chain analysis using hybrid simulation and AHP. *International Journal of Production Economics* 105, 536-547.

Reichert, A. K., Cho, C. -C., Wagner, G. M. (1983). An examination of the conceptual issues involved in developing credit scoring models. *Journal of Business and Economic Statistics* 1, 101–114.

Reid, E., Qin, W., Chung, W., Xu, J., Zhou, Y., Schumaker, R., Sageman, M., Chen, H. (2004). Terrorism knowledge discovery project: A knowledge discovery approach to addressing the threats of terrorism, *Proceedings of the Second Symposium on Intelligence and Security Informatics*. Tucson: University of Arizona, pp. 125-145.

Reilly, L.A., Courtenay, O. (2007). Husbandry practices, badger sett density and habitat composition as risk factors for transient and persistent bovine tuberculosis on UK cattle farms, *Preventive Veterinary Medicine* 80:2-3, pp. 129-142.

Rice, B, Caniato, F. (2003). Supply chain response to terrorism: Creating resilient and secure supply chains, *Supply Chain Response to Terrorism Project Interim Report*. Cambridge, MA: MIT Center for Transportation and Logistics.

Ritchie, B., Brindly, C. (2007). Supply chain risk management and performance: A guiding framework for future development, *International Journal of Operations & Production Management* 27:3, pp. 303-322.

Ryoo, J., Choi, Y.B. (2006). A comparison and classification framework for disaster information management systems, *International Journal of Emergency Management* 3:4, pp. 264-279.

Saaty, T.L. (1977). A scaling method for priorities in hierarchical structures. *Journal of Mathematical Psychology* 15, pp. 234-281.

Sahin, F., Robinson, E.P. (2002). Flow coordination and information sharing in supply chains: Review, implications, and directions for future research. *Decision Sciences* 33:4, pp. 505-536.

Salasznyk, P.P., Lee, E.E., List, G.F., Wallace, W.A. (2006). A systems view of data integration for emergency response, *International Journal of Emergency Management* 3:4, pp. 313-331.

Scandizzo, S. (2005). Risk mapping and key risk indicators in operational risk management. *Economic Notes by Banca Monte dei Paschi di Siena SpA* 34:2, pp. 231-256.

Schaefer, A, Cassidy, M., Marshall, K., Rossi, J. (2006), Internal audits and executive education: A holy alliance to reduce theft and misreporting, *Employee Relations Law Journal* 32:1, pp. 61-84.

Sereda, H. Gaudio, D. Tait, E. (2005) RMIS: Taking data management enterprisewide, *Risk Management Magazine* October, pp. 42-52.

Sharpe, W.F. (1964). Capital asset prices: A theory of market equilibrium under conditions of risk, Journal of Finance, 19(3), pp. 425-442.

Smaltz, D.H., Carpenter, R., Saltz, J. (2007). Effective IT governance in healthcare organizations: A tale of two organizations, *International Journal of Healthcare Technology and Management* 8:1/2, pp. 20-41.

Sobehart, J., Keenan, S. (2001). Measuring Default Accurately, *Credit Risk Special Report, Risk* 14, pp. 31–33.

Stapleton, G., Rezak, C.J. (2004). Change management underpins a successful ERP implementation at Marathon Oil, *Journal of Organizational Excellence* 23:4, pp. 15-22.

Sterman, J.D. (1989). Modeling managerial behavior: misperceptions of feedback in a dynamic decision making experiment, *Management Science* 35:3, pp. 321-339.

Steuer, R.E. (1986). *Multiple Criteria Optimization: Theory, Computation, and Application.* New York: John Wiley & Sons.

Suder, G., Gillingham, D.W. (2007). Paradigms and paradoxes of agricultural risk governance, *International Journal of Risk Assessment and Management* 7:3, pp. 444-457.

Talluri, S., Narasimhan, R., Nair, A. (2006), Vendor performance with supply risk: A chance-constrained DEA approach. *International Journal of Production Economics* 100, pp. 212-222.

Tan, W.-J., Enderwick, P. (2006). Managing threats in the global era: The impact and response to SARS, *Thunderbird International Business Review* 48:4, pp. 515-536.

Tang, C.S. (2006a). Perspectives in supply chain risk management, *International Journal of Production Economics* 103, pp. 451-488.

Tang, C.S. (2006b). Robust strategies for mitigating supply chain disruptions, *International Journal of Logistics: Research and Applications* 9:1, pp. 33-45.

Taylor, N. (2007). A note on the importance of overnight information in risk management models. *Journal of Banking & Finance* 31, pp. 161-180.

Tchokogué, A., Bareil, C., Duguay, C.R. (2005). Key lessons from the implementation of an ERP at Pratt & Whitney Canada, *International Journal of Production Economics* 95, pp. 151-163.

Thomas, D.J., Griffin, P.M. (1996). Coordinated supply chain management. European Journal of Operational Research 94:1, pp. 1-15.

Thomas L. C. (2000). A survey of credit and behavioural scoring: forecasting financial risk of lending to consumers. *International Journal of Forecasting*, 16: 2149-172.

Thompson, S., Altay, N., Green, W.G. III, Lapetina, J. (2006). Improving disaster response efforts with decision support systems, *International Journal of Emergency Management* 3:4, pp. 250-263.

United States General Accounting Office (2003). Homeland security: Efforts to improve information sharing need to be strengthened, *Report to the Secretary of Homeland Security*. Washington: GAO-03-760.

VanderBok, R., Sauter, J.A., Bryan, C, Horan, J. (2007). Manage your supply chain risk, *Manufacturing Engineering* 138:3, 153-153-156, 158, pp. 160-161.

Van Everdingen, Y., van Hellegersberg, J., Waarts, E. (2000). ERP adoption by European midsize companies, *Communications of the ACM* 43:4, pp. 27-31.

Van Mieghem, J., Dada, M. (2001). Price versus production postponement: Capacity and competition, *Management Science* 45, pp. 1631-1649.

Vergin, R.C. (1998). An examination of inventory turnover in the fortune 500 industrial companies, *Production and Inventory Management Journal* 39, pp. 51-56.

von Bertalanffy, L. (1968). *General System Theory: Foundations, Development, Applications*, New York: George Brazillier, Inc., revised 1969.

Wade, J. (2007). The bittersweet poison in the prescription drug supply chain, *Risk Management* 54:7, p. 12.

Wagner, H. (2004). The use of credit scoring in the mortgage industry. *Journal of Financial Services Marketing* 9:2, pp. 179-183.

Wald, J., Holleran, J. (2007). Counterfeit products and faulty supply chain, *Risk Management* 54:4, pp. 58-62.

Walden, J., Kaplan, E.H. (2004). Estimating time and size of a bioterror attack, *Emergency Infectious Disease* 1:7.

Walker, L., Shenkir, W.G., Barton, T.L. (2003). ERM in practice 60:4, pp. 51-55.

Waller, M., Johnson, J.E., Davis, T. (1999). Vendor-Managed Inventory in the retail supply chain, *Journal of Business Logistics*, 20:1, pp. 183-203.

Wang, J., Shu, Y.-F. (2007). A possibilistic decision model for new product supply chain design. *European Journal of Operational Research* 177, 1044-1061.

Weimann, G. (2004). *How Modern Terrorism Uses the Internet.* Washington, DC: United States Institute of Peace, Special Report No. 116.

Williamson, M. (1997). From SAP to 'nuts?' *Computerworld* 31:45, Nov. 10, pp. 68-69.

Woltjer, R., Lindgren, I., Smith, K. (2006). A case study of information and communication technology in emergency management training, *International Journal of Emergency Management* 3:4, pp. 332-347.

Woudenberg, F. (1991). An evaluation of Delphi, *Technological Forecasting and Social Change*, September.

Wu, D., Olson, D.L. (2007). A comparison of stochastic dominance and stochastic DEA for vendor evaluation. *International Journal of Production Research* to be published.

Wynstra, F., VanWeele, FA., Weggemann, M. (2001). Managing supplier involvement in product development: Three critical issues, *European Management Journal* 19:2, 157-167.

Xu, K., Dong, Y. (2004). Information gaming in demand collaboration and supply chain performance, *Journal of Business Logistics* 25:1, pp. 121-144.

Zsidisin, G.A., Smith, M.E. (2005). Managing supply risk with early supplier involvement: A case study and research propositions, *The Journal of Supply Chain Management* Fall, pp. 44-56.

Index